The Positioning Manual for Indie Consultants

Philip Morgan

IBEX
PUBLISHING

Ibex Publishing
Taos, NM

Bulk Orders
philip@philipmorganconsulting.com

First Edition, 2021

Library of Congress Control Number: 2021904493

ISBN: 978-1-7367975-0-1

Dedicated to those who, out of desire to serve, are willing to press the publish button before they are certain.

CONTENTS

Acknowledgments

I owe a debt of gratitude to many people for helping with this book.

My wife, Cheryl, whose love, patience, and encouragement has been essential, and who has given me an invaluable window into a world where sunk costs almost never interfere with moving forward in life.

The trees, creeks, and landscape of Carson National Forest near Taos, NM, that lent me sanity and calm during a personally difficult time.

My parents, who filled our home with books and music, helped me learn to question, drove me countless times to the Mocksville public library and the far better ones in Forsythe County, and created enough stability at home that I didn't leave there a broken person. These are priceless gifts and privileges that live on in me today.

Jonathan Stark, for challenging me to specialize years ago.

Blair Enns, whose *Win Without Pitching Manifesto* was an impactful experience that supplied me with the concepts I needed to begin exploring the domain of specialization.

David C. Baker, who has long offered warm support for my work and who included me in a wonderful writing retreat in late 2019 that helped push this book over the finish line.

Simon Wardley, who has generously shared and furiously advocated a helpful and democratizing way of thinking about business strategy and in so doing, has modeled an approach to leadership I find incredibly inspiring.

Sarah A., Ian C., Eric W., James S., Thai W., Bernhard W., Aaron S., Liston W., Nadia C., Kerry N., Tom K., Neeraj H., John H., Leah W., Rob W., Hamza G., Ben

W., Martin R., Lee B., Keanan K., Amit S., Curtis C., David S., Rob S., Drew U., Judd L., Aleth G., Andrew C., Aylwin S., Luke D., Craig D., Jonathan B., Atul P., Michael P., Gustavo N., and Gary H., for agreeing individually to beta read and collectively to convince me to throw away a well-intentioned but overdone first start to make way for something better.

And finally, I thank the 2,154 readers of the previous editions of this manual, especially all those who wrote with thoughtful and challenging questions that helped me pierce the epidermis of expertise on this topic so I could bring you this much improved version of the manual. I couldn't have done it without y'all. Thank you.

Introduction

The ability that fundamentally transforms the career of an independent consultant is an ability to earn new visibility and trust. If you want to transform your business and career for the better, you need to focus on getting better at earning visibility and trust.

This seems simple, but asking *how* we get better at earning visibility and trust— with all of the apparent complexities of modern marketing and all the bullshit advice out there about it—opens a can of worms. Over the course of this book, we're going to do whatever it is you do to make the problem of an opened can of worms go away. (Do you eat them? Release them into the wild? I've never inquired.) In our case, we're going to tackle, make sense of, and help you answer the question of how *you* can get better at earning visibility and trust.

Along the way, we'll need to explore and understand the ideas of specialization and positioning, because without specialization, getting better at earning visibility and trust is an excessively difficult, unfocused slog. We'll also need to understand how to cultivate valuable expertise in the unstructured world of independent consulting, which exists outside of the more structured, controlled world of the licensed professions.

This book is titled *The Positioning Manual for Indie Consultants* because it's the most comprehensive resource on positioning for you (if you're an indie consultant), because it's a significant evolution of an existing book that has some brand equity I'd like to preserve by avoiding a drastic name change, and because it's a far better title than *The Earning Visibility and Trust Manual for Indie Consultants*.

Let's begin our inquiry into how you earn visibility and trust; an extremely productive endeavor that also generates transformative answers to other important business strategy questions you should be asking.

Section 1

How You Earn Visibility

Effortless Visibility

There's this guy named Matt Cutts. There was a five-year period of time when if Matt Cutts published something about a certain topic, well over 50,000 people cared about what he said. They cared immediately, deeply, and sometimes angrily.

That's visibility. A rather extreme level of visibility, in fact.

To get that level of visibility, Matt Cutts was merely good at his job for 17 years. That job was a high-profile position in the areas of web spam and search quality at Google.

Matt became an unofficial spokesperson who explained and defended the often-opaque changes Google made to its search engine algorithm. If you needed to understand these periodic algorithm changes and what impact they might have, you paid attention to Matt Cutts.

Two kinds of people had skin in the game here: people (or companies) with content that ranked well in a Google search, and people who wanted to improve how their clients' content ranked in a Google search. The latter are often called search engine optimizers (SEOs).

The latter is where I get my "well over 50,000 people" number from. According to statista.com, at the time of this writing there are more than 13,300 ad agencies, and from that point, it's a reasonable extrapolation to 50K people who care about SEO, and therefore, 50K people who care what the unofficial spokesperson for the most powerful search algorithm on the planet has to say about SEO. That's not counting the large number of people or businesses who would be personally affected by changes to Google's search algorithm, and therefore, would also care about Matt Cutts' explanation of those changes.

If Matt Cutts had become an indie consultant after he left his job at Google in 2017, he would have instantly become the single most visible and authoritative consultant in the SEO world.

He would have expended zero effort earning visibility and would have the most visibility an indie consultant could possibly ask for.

Inherited Fame

There are cases where earning visibility just happens without you trying at all.

You could inherit an extreme amount of visibility the way Matt Cutts did.

Thinking of this as "niche fame" is pretty accurate because fame itself is an extreme form of visibility.

You could inherit niche fame from a parent, the way children of celebrities or royalty do.

Or, you could have an incredibly productive professional or personal network and be so visible within that network that the ratio of opportunity-to-visibility is so favorable that you are effectively niche famous within your network.

All of the above do happen out there in the world, and the visibility is not earned; it's *inherited*.

Most of us, however, are not Matt Cutts, are not children of celebrities, and have a sorta-okay network. We eventually reach a point where we've extracted most of the opportunity our sorta-okay network is going to yield. No matter how good we are at helping our clients with strategy or execution, we tend to wait until a moment of crisis to consider changing how we earn visibility for ourselves or our business. We all know the saying about the best time to plant a tree, and yet we wait until we'd like some almonds to satiate our hunger before we think about planting an almond tree.

When speaking aloud the phrase "do marketing," I will almost always use air quotes, because to me, you don't "do marketing" any more than a single person can "do marriage." Marketing is a relationship in service of change, or more pragmatically, marketing is the process of cultivating the relationships that help you earn visibility and trust from a market.

We reach this crisis—this unsustainable moment in our business—and decide we need to "do marketing." When we say "I need to do marketing," we are really saying "I need to work at earning new visibility for my business."

Matt Cutts did his job well and inherited an immense amount of visibility as a second-order consequence.

We need to learn to do a good job of earning visibility, and as a second-order consequence, we do our jobs as indie consultants better.

Chapter 1: What Is Marketing?

Marketing is earning visibility and trust for your service offerings, business, or thinking. There are other definitions, of course, for marketing.

Seth Godin would define it, very poetically, as changing the culture.

Management: Tasks, Responsibilities, Practices by Peter F. Drucker

Peter Drucker wrote that "the aim of marketing is to make selling superfluous. The aim of marketing is to know and understand the customer so well that the product or service fits him and sells itself."

The American Marketing Association definition: "Marketing is the process of planning and executing the conception, pricing, promotion, and distribution of ideas, goods, and services to create exchanges that satisfy individual and organizational goals."

If we try to navigate the Scylla and Charybdis that these definitions represent (too abstract and too specific) and get to a definition that works for indie consultants, we end up pretty close to my definition: "Marketing is earning visibility and trust for your service offerings, business, or thinking."

Your Business Might Have Been Born in a Cradle Called Crisis

My definition creates tension because it presupposes a proactive context and a relaxed timeframe. It presupposes that you've begun the work of earning visibility and trust well before you need the results of that work. The reality is that for most of us, our interest in marketing is born during a moment of crisis in our business. A cradle of crisis.

Crisis: a time of great danger, difficulty, or confusion when problems must be solved or important decisions must be made.

Source: *Oxford Advanced American Dictionary*

Usually, it's the famine phase of the feast-famine cycle that creates this crisis. During this moment, the idea of patiently, generously *earning* our way out of the crisis into a more stable condition isn't the most palatable idea. We are poorly supplied with both the time and resources needed to earn visibility and trust in a way that signals to the market that we are the custodian of rare, valuable expertise. I've been there myself, and I have a visceral memory of the unique stench of this flavor of desperation.

This crisis moment leads us to look for faster-acting solutions. And boy, do we find them!

Wherever we happen to look for our answers about how to "do marketing," if our desired timeline to results is months rather than years, we filter for a category of answers that is known as direct response marketing.

Direct Response Marketing

Direct response marketing is a button or form with a funnel behind it.

If you are camping in the wilderness at night, and from the warmth of your sleeping bag you hear an animal outside the tent, you'll listen closely to determine whether it's a bird, a small mammal, or something you need to actually be worried about. Below are the "bird calls" of direct response marketing.

"To get the free bonus, send me your Amazon receipt showing that you've prepurchased 10 or more copies of my book." (This is a call to action, or a CTA.)

"To receive this free email course, tell me what email address to send it to." (This is a low-friction form used to collect signups or opt-ins.)

"To download this white paper, please tell us about your company demographics and needs." (This is a gated content asset.)

"Buy this $7 e-book and learn how to increase your website's conversion rate." (This is a low-priced product used to measure buying intent and collect contact information.)

"Attend this free webinar and learn how to price your services more profitably." (This is an event used to collect contact information that will later be used to promote something.)

These are the "bird calls"—the *language* of direct response marketing. Direct response marketing may also make use of the following:

- Long form sales copy

- A sequence of emails that describes some pain or problem, spends time vivifying that pain/problem, and pitches a solution to that pain/problem

- Money-back guarantees

- Testimonials

- Engineered pricing (a price schedule with three or more tiers designed to maximize volume, revenue, or profitability)

The genre of heavy metal music prepares you to hear distorted electric guitars, heavy drumming, and screamed vocals. There is a fun subgenre of novelty heavy metal music. In that subgenre, you have groups like Hayseed Dixie playing AC/DC songs on guitar, mandolin, banjo, and fiddle in bluegrass style. The difference is not the notes being played, it's the entire *tone* of the resulting music.

Direct response marketing also has a certain tone to it:

- The goal of direct response marketing is to *get a response* from those we market to. This is the most fundamental, defining aspect of the genre. The "response" is not necessarily a sale. It might be some other kind of action: filling out a form, clicking a button, opening an email, attending an event, joining a waiting list, or the like. **The larger goal of direct response marketing is to produce measurable results quickly, in weeks or months, rather than years**.

- The ethos of direct response marketing is creating a personalized, one-to-one connection with prospects from the very first interaction.

- Direct response marketing will intentionally or accidentally collect data—the more individualized and complete the better—about prospects.

- Critically, direct response marketing is focused on *problems*.

- Direct response marketing often tries to manufacture or amplify *urgency* around the recipient taking some kind of action.

- A lot of direct response marketing focuses on the *pain* of the problem the marketer purports to solve. The pain of doing nothing. The pain of doing the wrong thing.

- Sometimes you'll see direct response marketing make use of *curiosity*. The apotheosis of curiosity in direct response marketing is the clickbait headline.

- Product or service benefits will often be stated in strong or exaggerated ways in direct response marketing.

The Danger of the Wrong Tools in the Wrong Context

Eighty percent of the results returned to a search for *marketing for consultants* will be advice about how to implement direct response marketing. There's nothing wrong with this, but let's recognize both the content and the context at play here.

Excluding the results for marketing agency services, that is.

The *content* of your search for advice about how to "do marketing" for a consultant is dominated by advice about how to implement direct response marketing. That's because the *context* surrounding most of these searches is: "Holy crap, I need more work NOW NOW NOW and my network isn't coughing up opportunity like it used to and OH MY GOD, I NEED WORK NOW WHAT DO I DO?!?!?!" Maybe that's not *you* right now, but the folks writing the advice and working to get it ranking well on SERP pages are aware of the searcher's likely context, and so all the incentives align to supply the searcher for *marketing for consultants* with direct response-oriented advice.

Direct response marketing is . . . fine. It's morally fine, and it represents a neutral set of marketing tools that can be useful and effective.

However, using direct response marketing tools in a context of desperation or impatience is fundamentally incompatible with the idea that you have cultivated rare, valuable expertise. It threatens your reputation as an expert. That's the only reason I spent the previous

Would you trust a brain surgeon whose website tried to get you to download an e-book on the seven benefits of brain surgery? (This example is exaggerated, of course, to point out the underlying tension between having rare, valuable expertise and needing the opportunity to apply it. If you have the former, we expect you to have an abundance of opportunity as well.)

~700 words talking about direct response marketing. If this tool set combined with impatience or desperation wasn't a threat to your reputation in the marketplace, I wouldn't bother defining it for you. But, because we tend to be in a moment of crisis when we first seek out advice about marketing, this stuff about direct response marketing matters and recognizing the "bird calls" of direct response marketing is valuable for us.

The Right Tools

The alternative to direct response marketing is brand marketing.

Brand marketing is a gift with a logo on it.

I'm not going to try to further define brand marketing here because brand marketing is the mindset and approach that informs every bit of this book.

Brand marketing is actually a bit harder to define, and I really believe that you'll be better served by soaking up the idea of it, the *feeling* of it, through the rest of this book. Which, by the way, *really is* about specialization and positioning for indie consultants! This detour through what marketing in general is—and what direct response and brand marketing specifically are—was necessary context to help you get the most possible out of what follows in this book.

Visibility Is Central to Marketing

Again, marketing is earning visibility and trust for your service offerings, business, or thinking.

If you're invisible to your prospects, they can't trust you for obvious reasons. So marketing starts with answering the question: How do I earn visibility?

In marketing, there is a multitude of small ideas that huddle together under the big umbrella of *visibility*. You've probably heard the labels for some of these small ideas: lead generation, reach, audience size, stages of awareness, and so on. I thank the branding and marketing firm Hinge Marketing for popularizing an idea that lets us unify all these small ideas under the umbrella of a big, powerful idea: *visibility*.

Buyers can't buy from you if they don't know you exist. They can't trust you if they don't know you exist. They can't evaluate whether you are trustworthy if they don't know you exist.

Visibility—being seen by your market—is the precondition to every downstream necessity in marketing.

I'll henceforth assume that you, like 98 percent of us, need to plan and work to earn visibility because it's not automatic for you like it was for Matt Cutts, and like it is for the children of celebrities.

Let's methodically and thoroughly answer the "How do I earn visibility?" question.

Chapter 2: The Platformer Advantage

Our first move when facing the "How do I earn visibility?" question (the HDIEV question) is to examine the landscape around us and observe what others are doing to earn visibility. As we do, we will first notice others who have inherited or lucked their way into visibility, and then we will notice those who are successful at *intentionally* earning visibility.

Among those who are successful at earning visibility, there are two subgroups. The first is like my acquaintance Stacy.

Stacy had a great business teaching designers how to build strategy into their service offerings. Then Stacy started using a new project management SaaS (software as a service). The SaaS product is quite difficult to learn, but Stacy really liked it and published a few videos on how to use it.

The videos went viral. Stacy casually mentioned that she was building on a course that goes deeper into how to use this difficult product.

This should remind you a bit of Matt Cutts, but without the employee dynamic at play with him and Google.

Stacy now makes more money selling this course than from teaching designers how to build strategy into their service offerings. The SaaS platform owner has recruited Stacy as a tech evangelist for the product.

Stacy is a *platformer*. A very visible one.

For our purposes, a platform can be:

- A business process framework (i.e., EOS, 3HAG, Six Sigma, Agile, Lean, TDD)

- A programming language (i.e., Python, Ruby, C#)

- A software framework (i.e., React, VueJS, Laravel)

- An actual platform you can build stuff on (i.e., AWS, Linux, Windows, Salesforce)

A platform is a "thing," often, but not always, a product that lots of businesses use and need help understanding, planning for, implementing, operating, extending, supporting, fixing, optimizing, and upgrading—like the project management SaaS that Stacy became an expert on.

Among those who are successful at earning visibility, platformers are our first subgroup. Our second subgroup is everybody else, and we'll examine them later.

"I'm flying, Jack!"
– Rose DeWitt Bukater, *Titanic*

As we study platformers, we notice that their visibility is linked to the platform itself in many ways. While the platform is actually an idea, framework, or software product, the platform is also a *thing* that you can stand on and use to earn visibility. The platform is infrastructure that lifts you above the crowd and makes you more visible.

Platform Performance Characteristics

The infrastructure of a platform can take many forms. Here are some of the most common ones.

Directories of preferred, certified, or authorized vendors. My acquaintance Stacy encountered the new, difficult-to-learn project management SaaS before it created a directory of vendors who can help implement it, but if this SaaS platform is like most, it will eventually create a vendor directory. Others will get the kind of visibility boost that Stacy has from the platform, though without the first-mover advantage that Stacy enjoys.

Platform vendor directories reduce search cost and promise to reduce risk via the vetting we presume the platform does on those listed in the directory; prospects are incentivized to discover and use the directory if they need help understanding, planning for, implementing, operating, extending, supporting, fixing, optimizing, or upgrading the platform. And vendors are incentivized to get themselves listed in the directory to benefit from this low-cost visibility boost.

Communities and events. Salesforce reports that over 171,000 people attended their flagship conference Dreamforce in 2019, and over 16 million people viewed the event online. Sixty-eight people delivered keynote talks, and we can safely assume the speakers were not able to assemble such a large audience without the help of the Salesforce platform.

Platforms attract communities of users, and those users have needs. By also joining and serving those communities, platformers can earn visibility more easily than if the platform did not exist.

Whole product ecosystem. Geoffrey A. Moore has given language to a strategic play that a lot of vendors implement; helping risk-averse clients adopt the platform by making the core product into what Moore calls a *whole product*—the core product (Salesforce, for example) combined with all the other stuff that risk-averse companies need to successfully use it, including:

Crossing the Chasm: Marketing and Selling High-Tech Products to Mainstream Customers

- Standards and best practices
- Service providers who know how to plan, implement, and support the core product
- Integrations with other products the user may depend on
- Training to help the user get more value from—or reduce the pain of using—the core product

Indie consultants who are platformers can assist the platform vendor with every single one of those parts of the whole product ecosystem. Stacy helped the difficult-to-use project management SaaS by creating training content. It doesn't matter that Stacy owns this content rather than the platform vendor, because as long as the training is available within the whole product ecosystem, the platform vendor gets access to a larger more risk-averse market than they otherwise

If you're feeling a low-level sense of discomfort about whether this win-win balance can persist over the long-term given the asymmetry in size between Stacy and the platform vendor, your instincts are good.

would. Stacy is happy, and the platform vendor is happy.

In the early days, the difficult-to-use project management SaaS vendor needs to remain focused on their core product, so they have every incentive to partner formally or informally with those who show up to contribute to their whole product ecosystem. Curious, ambitious folks like Stacy who figure out best practices early or create training content will be embraced. Services firms who start offering support for the platform will be freely sent opportunity.

"These were the happy days; the salad days as they say."
– H.I. McDunnough, *Raising Arizona*

During this time, the platform vendor is incentivized to leverage the perceived objectivity of indie consultants. Their platform is new and poorly understood by the market. When a third party (you, maybe!) shows up with published content that explains or analyzes the platform and presents it in even a mildly favorable light, they will amplify your content by sharing it. Even if you have more visibility than the new platform does, this can help further expand your visibility. The platform vendor is striving for greater visibility in the market too, and so in those early days of the platform, platformers gain an informal "visibility partner" from the platform itself.

Finally, we can't ignore the simple physics of market size. Adopting a new platform involves *change*, and change creates new problems. For our platformers, every new customer that adopts the platform they are focused on is a potential new customer for their consulting services. The platform is actively working to expand its market size, and that expands the market size for indie consultants who have specialized in that platform.

This moment in the platform's evolution—which can easily be a three to five-year-long moment—is a beautiful one. The platform is growing and spinning off opportunity for platformers, and the platformer's efforts at gaining expanded visibility benefit both themselves and the platform. Everybody is winning all the time.

As indie rock podcaster John Roderick likes to say about that moment when a new band is blowing up, "Every time the phone rings it's more good news."

The Role of Platform Latecomers

Word gets around about this place in the market where the salad days are happening. The "Oakies" in less fertile parts hear about it, and they migrate to the promised land of this new, vibrant, growing platform.

Additionally, no platform—no matter how large it ultimately becomes—needs an *infinite* supply of whole product support. At some point, there is enough training, and potential standards and best practices have converged on a right-sized corpus of guidance. At some point, there are *enough* vendors to provide good-enough quality planning, implementation, and support for the platform.

While there may always be room for new approaches to fitting into the whole product ecosystem, at some point, the predominant story becomes *equilibrium* rather than *growth*. Commoditization rather than exploration and customization. Efficiency and reliability rather than innovation.

"All good things come to an end."
– Chaucer

"All good things ~~come to an end~~ become commodities."
– Philip Morgan

The eighth and ninth wonders of the world are compounding interest and commoditization.

Commoditization is why, if a car breaks down, it can be fixed in days rather than weeks or months. The mechanic can order an off-the-shelf part that drops right in. No craftsman is involved; instead, it's engineers, CAD, precision manufacturing, and sophisticated distribution.

Commoditization is why there is the concept of middle management. It is why we plug devices into a power socket or Ethernet connection and they just work. I'm convinced that commoditization equals compounding interest as the other most powerful human-invented force on the planet.

Commoditization is a good thing for humans.

Commoditization is a bad thing for platformers.

The early years of a platform are years of growth, innovation, and opportunity. The salad days.

As the platform matures into commoditization, the salad wilts, at least for those who have businesses that are optimized for growth, innovation, and that sort of thing. Imagine raising a human child on a diet rich in fat and carbohydrates and then when they become a teenager, the only food available to them are salads with no fatty salad dressing. That would be one hell of an adjustment. They would probably live, but they'd hate every minute of this new diet they'd be forced to eat.

This is what commoditization does to a platform ecosystem. As the predominant story becomes equilibrium rather than growth, it forces change on all members of the ecosystem. Both the platform and the indie consultants, hanging off it like baby possums off their mother, are forced to change.

What Happens When the King Gets Hungry

If you would like an image to set the tone for what's next, search for the painting "Saturn Devouring His Son" by Francisco Goya.

Once a platform reaches that equilibrium state, growth often starts to level off. Usually, the platform (if we personify it as a person rather than as a business) starts to look around for new sources of revenue or profitability. The king gets hungry.

For a stable platform, the next wave of innovation is often not the product itself, but new forms of monetizing the product or the product's customer base. This "second-wave innovation" may take one or more of the following forms:

- **Vertical integration**, by adding a services division.

- **Bigger clients**, and raising the bar for partners ("*Pffft!* We can talk about *gold partner status* when you've brought us five $50K projects").

Examples: unbundling and charging for the now-unbundled component, moving important functionality out of lower priced tiers and into higher ones.

- **Pure rent-seeking** stuff that pisses off customers and weakens the customer segment that you, an indie consultant, depend on.

This "second-wave innovation" couples with what has already been happening without the platform's direct involvement; the aforementioned increase in supply of whole product ecosystem componentry. The "Oakies" in less fertile platform ecosystems hear about the growing, vibrant platform ecosystem and they migrate to the promised land. The supply of talent increases at the same time the platform itself begins sharing the opportunity the ecosystem offers less generously.

At this point, our platformers have a choice—to fundamentally change their business from one that thrives in dynamic, expanding ecosystem to one that thrives in a stable, fixed ecosystem. The former is a business that can "figure shit out" and get paid for doing so; the latter is a business that can deliver quality with high consistency and low cost. Innovative versus efficient. Those are two *very* different kinds of businesses, and evolving from one into the other is not easy.

Many platformers will choose to migrate to another younger platform instead of evolving from an innovative "figure shit out" business to an efficient commodity business. They're starting over, but in an environment where the question of how they earn visibility has a familiar answer.

Some platforms, it should be said, end up like the *RMS Titanic*. They die a sudden death that takes many of the businesses that were riding atop it down to a watery death.

Other platformers will attempt the difficult evolution from an innovative to an efficient business. They will choose that route rather than migrate to a different platform or figure out how to earn visibility without the help of a platform.

You can see, I hope, that during the salad days, the platform is delighted to help you solve your visibility problem in exchange for help with their whole product ecosystem problem.

As the salad beings to wilt, the king gets hungry and starts to alter the deal. If you are a platformer, you pray that he does not alter it further.

PLATFORM EVOLUTION

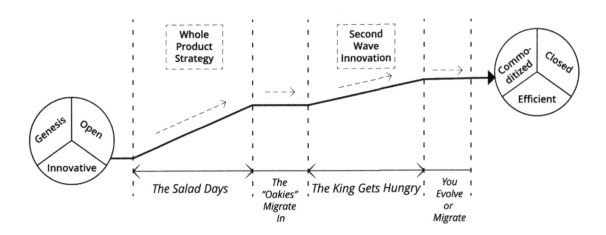

That's our first subgroup of businesses that are succeeding at visibility: platformers. Next, we'll look at the other subgroup.

Chapter 3: Earning Visibility Without a Platform

What about everybody else? Those who are not riding astride a platform?

When we look closer at the non-platformers, we see two subgroups. The first seems to have some kind of external infrastructure they use to earn visibility. So does the second, but the second group has built their own infrastructure for visibility. We can think of the first group as using off-the-shelf rented infrastructure to earn visibility, and the second as building their own infrastructure.

Rented Infrastructure

I have a client who generates about $400,000 a year in consulting revenue. He employs one assistant, works out of a small home office, and has no website. He spends a lot of time on other people's stages, though, speaking at conferences and other events. He uses their "infrastructure" to earn a significant amount of visibility for his work.

He doesn't "own" this infrastructure the way he would own his website or email list, but he has good access that allows him to use other people's infrastructure to create economic value for his business. The conferences, communities, and events that other people have convened are a good example of *external infrastructure* that indie consultants can use to earn visibility.

Media properties are another good example. These include trade publications which can range from print to pure online publications like a podcast, website, or YouTube channel. Often, these media properties are owned and operated by industry associations. You can see a quick example at nam.org, the National Association of Manufacturers. It's both a marketing site for the association and a media property that (hopefully) provides valuable content for the manufacturing industry. Some of that content will come from NAM employees and partners, and some will come from indie consultants who contribute articles, reports, white papers, and similar content in hopes of earning new visibility from the ~14,000 member companies that NAM represents.

Sometimes the external infrastructure is less formal— but not less substantial—when non-platformers partner with other businesses to earn visibility. Those other business may have a similar business model. One indie consultant partnering with another to earn more visibility. Peer businesses, in other words.

Those other businesses may have a very different business model. An indie consultant friend of mine does a lot of public speaking, mostly on stages at conferences for the industry he serves, but sometimes he speaks at online events for an audience-driven businesses like thefutur.com. My friend's business model is quite different than The Futur's model (an online education platform for creative entrepreneurs), so they're not peer businesses, but he benefits from the visibility that he earns from the external infrastructure The Futur provides him access to.

DIY Infrastructure

The other subgroup within the non-platformers group has built their own infrastructure for earning visibility. They might have done this out of preference, lack of access to external infrastructure, or in combination with access to external infrastructure. DIY infrastructure is not an either–or proposition.

They may have figured out how to help search engines like Google connect people who need answers with their website. Search engine optimization, in other words.

They may have built an email list of people who are interested in hearing from the consultant and they send free articles meant to provide value to this list.

They may have created their own community or events that help them earn visibility. Another indie consultant friend of mine convenes a CEO breakfast a few times a year. It's a sort of "pop-up community" sourced from his personal network and augmented by the personal networks of those he invites, and it regularly leads to greater visibility and opportunity for him.

Others have figured out how to use outreach—often with email or LinkedIn, but sometimes physical mail or the telephone network—to earn visibility. The ones who succeed here combine extensive research and an all-out effort at *relevance* in their outreach in order to earn visibility, and they tend to focus on what is known as a market vertical.

And yet others leverage the low barriers to connection, wide reach, and ability to casually strike up conversations on *social media* to earn visibility. These last two forms of DIY infrastructure—outreach and social media—do rely on external infrastructure, but that infrastructure is more like a utility or a toolbox; it is inert until it's used for some purpose.

To recap, the non-platformers who have succeeded at earning visibility for themselves fall into two subgroups:

1. External Infrastructure

- Conferences
- Events
- Communities
- Media properties
- Peer business partnerships
- Non-peer business partnerships

All of the above are "owned" by someone other than the indie consultant who is "renting" that infrastructure.

2. DIY Infrastructure

- Website
- Email list
- Community
- Events
- Outreach
- Social media

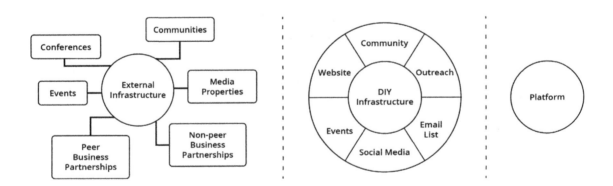

In the DIY subgroup, the consultant puts in the work to build up the infrastructure for visibility, and while they may not fully *control* the resulting community or social network, they "own" it more than those in the external infrastructure group do.

The Importance of Focus

What is generally true about these three groups—the platformers, the external infrastructure leveragers, and the DIY infrastructure builders? Two things.

1) The platformers seem to have the most help earning visibility. The platform does a lot of the work for them. The DIYers have the least help, and they do most of the visibility-earning work themselves by building their own infrastructure.

2) The non-platformers who are successful at earning visibility have made a decision about **focus**. That focus might be hyper narrow, or it might be somewhat broader, but the focus rarely is 100 percent generalist.

They have made this decision about focus because they *must*.

Attending **conferences or events** is a waste of time and money if they do not know *who* they are trying to connect with.

Participating in **communities** is awkward if there is no shared interest, so our non-platformers who are successful at earning visibility have invested in clarity about *what* they are interested in and willing to focus on.

Media properties are not interested in publishing their content if it is not relevant to the audience, so these non-platformers have learned *what* will make them relevant to an audience.

Google and other search engines easily connect searchers with useful web sites when it is clear *why* the website is a good match for someone's search intent, so our non-platformers have invested in this kind of focus and clarity on their website.

Useful outreach is differentiated from spam by the level of relevance in *who* it targets and *what* it offers them, so non-platformers who are successful at earning visibility through outreach invest the emotional labor needed to achieve genuine relevance.

We further burden our inbox by joining an **email list** when it is sufficiently clear *how* or *why* the list will produce value for us. Non-platformers also invest in this kind of relevance for their email list.

Non-platformers who are successful at earning visibility have invested in learning about *who* (they are trying to connect with), *what* (is relevant to them), and *why* (buyers will care enough to take action). This investment and learning leads them to *focus*. They cannot answer the foundational questions of visibility (who, what, why) if they do not focus in some way.

If *who* is everybody, and *what* is everything, then the answer to "Why would buyers want to know about you?" is: **they won't**.

Focus is necessary to create relevance, and relevance is the prerequisite to visibility.

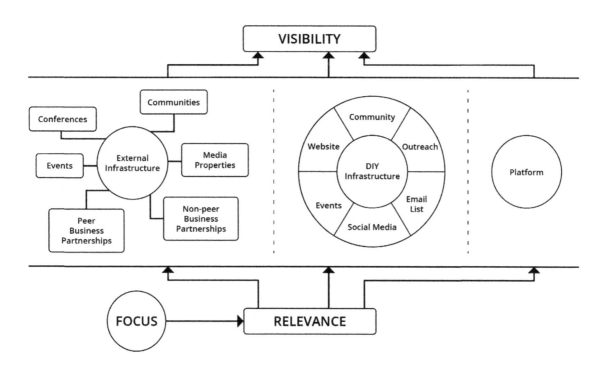

Chapter 4: A Model for Visibility

As we explore how earning visibility works, we're going to need a model to organize what we're seeing. When we look at the world of indie consultants who have succeeded at earning visibility, we see:

1. People who have effortlessly earned visibility (i.e., though not an indie consultant, Matt Cutts is a great example).

2. People who have focused on a platform (I've called them platformers).

3. People who have figured out how to use external infrastructure to earn visibility.

4. People who have built their own infrastructure for earning visibility.

We'll base our model on #2–4, because #1 is not a controllable, repeatable approach to earning visibility. Methods 2–4 are repeatable things any indie consultant can choose to do.

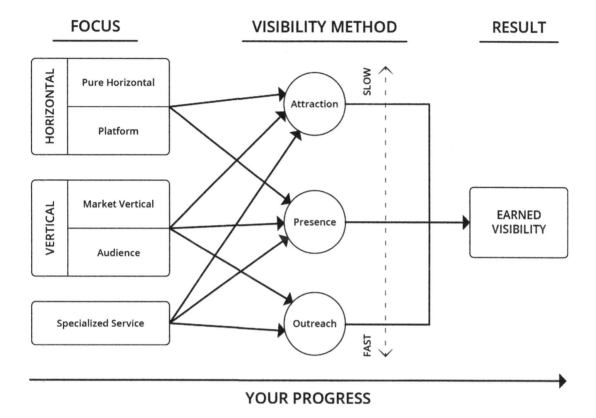

If you look at enough examples of indie consultants using a narrow focus to get better at earning visibility, you'll see five ways of focusing grouped into three categories:

- Vertical
    - Market Vertical
    - Audience
- Horizontal
    - Pure Horizontal

- Platform
- Service Specialization

Let's pile up the definitions we need right here so we can quickly get through them and on to more enjoyable and important stuff.

Wikipedia has a useful starting point definition I'll just borrow:

> A **vertical market** is a market in which vendors offer goods and services specific to an industry, trade, profession, or other group of customers with specialized needs. An example could be software that manages services in hotels—amenities solutions. It is distinguished from a **horizontal market** in which vendors offer a nonspecific, broad range of goods and services to a large group of customers with a wide range of needs, such as businesses as a whole, men, women, households, or, in the broadest horizontal market, everyone.

That's pretty good! Wikipedia is talking about *pure* market verticals and pure market horizontals. Market verticals and horizontals can range from incredibly narrow to quite broad. Within the seemingly narrow market vertical of "crushed and broken limestone mining and quarrying" (1,034 companies of this kind in the U.S.), there are 15 subcategories ranging from "agricultural limestone mining and/or beneficiating" to "riprap, limestone, mining, or quarrying." And, of course, there are very broad market verticals like "retail," "finance," and "education."

It's very informative to take a trip to www.naics.com/naics-drilldown-table/ and cruise around long enough to get a sense of the market verticals landscape. You'll be surprised how many there are that you've never even thought about.

An **audience** is a group of people or businesses that share something important in common. This shared problem, need, or goal is important enough that it causes the audience to connect and gather at online communities or in-person events. The fact that an audience *gathers* in some way makes them function like a pseudo vertical, and so both pure market verticals and audiences function as verticals.

I've discussed platforms already. To quickly recap, platforms are "things"—often, but not always, products—that a lot of businesses use and need help understanding, planning for, implementing, operating, extending, supporting, fixing, optimizing, and upgrading. A **platform specialization** is when an indie consultant provides services mostly or exclusively specialized in a certain platform.

A **pure horizontal specialization** is when you specialize in solving a specific problem or applying a specific form of expertise and you do not much care which business vertical or audience your clients come from. A client of mine helps start-ups craft a strategic narrative to improve employee alignment and velocity of innovation. His clients range from tech start-ups in the Seattle area to cosmetics brands that have just been absorbed into a larger conglomerate. He is a great example of a horizontal specialization.

Service specialization is where you specialize your service delivery. This is often synonymous with productization (where you standardize the scope and pricing of your services) or, more specifically, innovative service productization where you standardize your scope in a unique way that's attractive to a narrow spectrum of clients.

worstofalldesign.com/

One of my favorite examples of service specialization is Worstofall Design, which offers a one-day business branding service. The design of this productized service—along with how the service itself is branded—appeals to a narrow range of prospects, making the service more visible in the part of the market that is a good fit for the service.

A **multidimensional specialization** is when you combine both vertical and horizontal specializations. In reality, most specializations are multidimensional, because a hypothetically pure vertical specialization would mean you provide every possible service from cleaning toilets to executive coaching to a single vertical, and no company is ever really that unfocused (or versatile!).

Good Examples of Specialization

A few examples will help you identify these various specialization approaches when you encounter them in the wild. These are drawn from a necessarily incomplete but still helpful list I maintain at specializationexamples.com.

Pure Horizontal Focus

- **Voltage Control**: Design sprint workshops

- **The M. Ryan Group**: Inventory management

- **Maritz**: Employee motivation

Platform Focus

- **Dave Ceddia**: React training

- **The Duckbill Group**: AWS cost management

- **ABSYZ**: Salesforce consulting

Pure Vertical Focus

- **Hanno**: Digital products for health and wellness

- **IndustrialFX**: Digital marketing for manufacturing

- **Agrarian**: Digital marketing for New Zealand-based agribusinesses

Audience Focus

- **&Yet**: A digital marketing and dev shop firm focused on "weird" businesses

Things change on the internet. The examples below omit URLs for that reason, but the specializationexamples.com list includes live URLs and internet archive snapshots for these examples and others.

- **Urban Planet**: A dev shop focused on mission-driven organizations

- **Cher Hale**: PR for social good-focused companies

There are lots of amazing companies that could have just as easily been on this list of examples. Again, see more at specializationexamples.com.

Chapter 5: The Visibility Part of the Visibility Model

I've discussed the specialization part of the visibility model. It's also important to understand the visibility part. We've all seen companies create plans that omit a critical part of a process; testing as an afterthought to a software project, marketing as an afterthought to a product, and so on.

Specialization is a lever to help you get more out of your investment in visibility. The question of how you specialize and how you earn visibility are really two parts of the same thing. That's why they both exist within the same model.

To save you a little bit of page-flipping, here's our visibility model again:

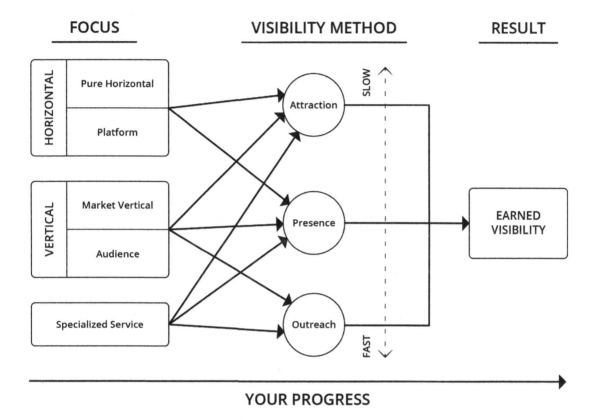

You'll notice there are three *methods* for earning visibility:

- **Outreach**: Contacting a stranger (via email, phone, mail, social media, etc.) to increase their visibility of your services. Can be automated and scaled using paid advertising or other methods. You initiate.

- **Presence**: Mingling and connecting with prospects. In other words, you *show up* in their world, physically or digitally. Often a bidirectional exchange that both increases your visibility and provides you deeper insight into their world.

- **Attraction**: A variety of methods that help interested prospects become aware of you. Usually, this happens by integrating somehow into their search for something—a solution to a problem, an answer to a question—although sometimes a random encounter creates new desire in a prospect. The prospect initiates.

These are actually *categories* of methods, and they are listed in descending order of how quickly they can earn you visibility; Outreach works the quickest and Attraction the slowest.

You'll also notice the lines connecting visibility methods with the three basic ways of specializing. Only one visibility method is incompatible with a way of specializing—visibility through outreach and horizontal specialization. Those two are largely incompatible.

Of course, there are exceptions to this. A smart, motivated, horizontally specialized consultant can find ways to make outreach work, but they will have to work at overcoming the fundamental incompatibility between the two. The other exception is certain platforms that *are* externally visible (CMS and CRM platforms are two such types), and as a result, outreach can be a viable way to earn visibility.

Horizontally specialized companies are usually focused on problems or opportunities that are not externally visible. Consider Maritz, which helps their clients with employee motivation. While it's reasonable to assume that almost every company would like their employees to be more motivated, an outreach campaign (direct unsolicited email, mail, phone calls, or LinkedIn messaging) from Maritz that assumes a *problematic* level of employee motivation would come across as insulting spam. This is why I generally consider outreach and horizontal specialization to be incompatible.

Timeline Considerations

If you need to earn more visibility for your services very quickly, you'll think about the five forms of specialization primarily through the lens of how fast-acting these three forms of earning visibility are, and perhaps choose a specialization approach based on its ability to leverage a fast-acting visibility mechanism. This means if you need to quickly earn more visibility for your services, you will avoid a horizontal specialization.

If fast-actingness were all there was to it, decision-making around specialization would be quite easy. But there is more to it. Notice the detail I've added to each visibility method.

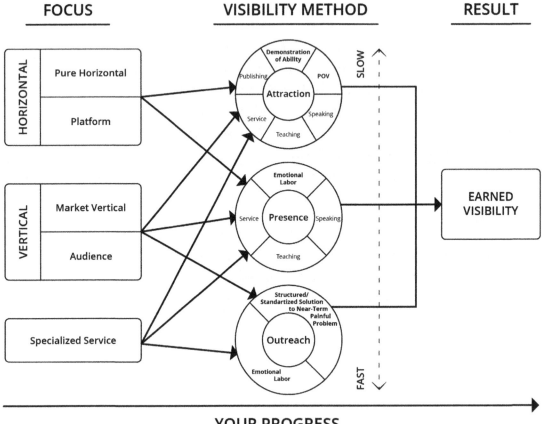

Fundamental Marketing Labor

Each category of visibility methods requires different types of *fundamental marketing labor* to make it work. For example, what makes Outreach effective is the emotional labor of caring about those you are reaching out to combined with offering a structured solution to an urgent—or at least, relevant—problem. If your personality does not afford you sufficient ability for emotional labor while earning visibility, you will want to avoid using the Outreach and Presence methods. If you tried to use Outreach anyway, you might get some quick wins, you might see others using Outreach effectively, or you might have some other short-term reason to do it, but it will be unsustainable because it requires something that is at odds with your personality.

A lot of marketing advice is focused on the choice of channel or platform. Email versus social media versus other stuff. The choice of channel/platform is secondary (and ephemeral over time), while the type of fundamental marketing labor is primary and more likely to be the same over time. Can't consistently perform emotional labor? That's fine, just don't choose Presence or Outreach, even if someone tells you one of those is the best thing since sliced bread. Got a knack for demonstrating ability, perhaps through public speaking? You'll gravitate toward Attraction and endure the slower acting-ness of this category of tools.

It's helpful, however, to link a few examples of channels or platforms with these three categories so that you can translate tactical marketing advice into strategic thinking about what might actually work for you.

- Attraction
  - Content marketing
  - Search engine optimization (SEO)
  - Blogging
  - Podcasting

As indie consultants, our personalities have an oversized influence on our businesses. In many cases, we can get assistance with things we hate doing. Bookkeeping comes to mind. But delegating emotional labor is nearly impossible, so any marketing approach that requires emotional labor is almost certainly going to have to be done by you.

Though paid advertising is a form of scaled Outreach without the requirement for emotional labor.

Most of the marketing advice you'll find on the internet is tactical in nature.

- Presence
    - Networking
    - Hosting a community
    - Social media interaction
- Outreach
    - LinkedIn messaging
    - Physical mail
    - Paid advertising

If you take only one thing away from this chapter, please let it be that while you can "mix and match" your method(s) for earning visibility and your way of specializing, they do form an integrated whole and need to be thought of in that way.

Chapter 6: The Importance of Thinking in Terms of Beachheads

How do we earn visibility for our business?

Well, at one level, we decide we *want* to do it, make a few decisions about *how*, and then implement those decisions. Simple!

The world, however, is a very large and complex place. To use a WWII metaphor, we are attempting to liberate Europe from the Axis armies, but taking on the whole continent all at once is impossible. We need a beachhead.

Specializing is choosing a beachhead, and almost all indie consultants who have become very visible to their prospects have specialized in some way.

www.naics.com/naics-drilldown-table/

The North American Industry Classification System (NAICS) is a good high-level map of the business world's terrain. It divides the world of business into top-level categories (i.e., Finance and Insurance, NAICS code 52), subcategories (i.e., Insurance Carriers, code 5241), and sub-subcategories (i.e., Reinsurance Carriers, code 524130).

There are 20 top-level categories and 422 bottom-level sub-subcategories. The bottom-level sub-subcategories range in size from eight establishments (Household Laundry Equipment Manufacturing) to 246,888 (Full-Service Restaurants) establishments. A graph of how many there are of each kind of business looks like this:

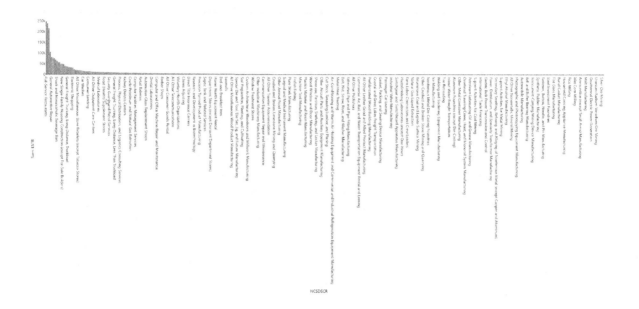

The detail of this graph is not very useful (that's why it's printed so small), but the overall distribution is interesting because it resembles a power law/long tail distribution.

The Right Size Beachhead

David C. Baker offers some well-researched guidelines for market size for small to mid-size professional services firms. A market with fewer than 2,000

www.davidcbaker.com/
how-man-competitors-
and-prospects-should-
you-have

prospective clients is too small; one with more than 10,000 is too large.

- 105 bottom-level NAICS categories fit David's right-size range (25 percent of the 422 sub-subcategories)

- 47 are too large (11 percent)

- 270 are too small (64 percent)

Of the sub-subcategories that are too small, many are subsets of a logical grouping that would *not* be too small to focus on. For example, Semiconductor and Related Device Manufacturing is a sub-subcategory with 863 establishments. Too small, but it is a subset of a group that includes PCB manufacturing, PCB assembly, and a few other related sub-subcategories. Grouping these together under the label Electronic Component Manufacturing makes sense and gets us focused on a sufficiently large market—a right-sized beachhead.

When you are defining a beachhead by grouping businesses together like this, what matters is not how you see the market, but *how the market sees itself*. Do semiconductor manufacturers see themselves as part of the same corner of the business ecosystem as PCB manufacturers and assemblers? Do they all identify with the same "extended business family"? If so, great, your label makes sense to them. If it doesn't, they'll see you as an out-of-touch outsider, which won't help you earn visibility from them.

The error most of us make when thinking about a beachhead is to misunderstand its role. The beachhead's role is not to provide 30 years' worth of opportunity to your business. To return to our WWII metaphor, the role of Normandy was not to contain and support the entire Allied invading army.

The role of a beachhead is to help you build up access and momentum that you can use to achieve a larger strategic goal. When you specialize to get better at earning visibility, you are choosing both a way of focusing (your larger strategic goal) and a way of building up access and momentum (your beachhead). The beachhead needs to be connected to the larger strategic goal, but the beachhead is just the beginning of a process that takes you to the larger goal.

Don't confuse your beachhead with your ultimate business goal.

Beachheads Are Not Face Tattoos

Beachheads are not permanent. The Allied armies did not invade Normandy, build some fortifications against the Axis armies still occupying the European continent, and then start roasting victory marshmallows on the beach.

Likewise, your decision about how to specialize—your "visibility beachhead"—is not a face tattoo; it is not permanent, especially in the early days.

A specialization is a decision about where and how you will focus your business. Eventually, a consistent specialization will become a *reputation*; the market will start to think of you in terms of your specialization. In the world of services, this is known as a *market position*.

If enough of the market thinks of you as focused on a certain market vertical, a certain horizontal (problem or platform), or a certain kind of service, then you have a market position.

Just like a reputation, your market position exists within the minds of those in the market. We do not live in the world depicted in the movie *The Matrix*, so it's not possible to "install" your reputation in every mind in the market all at once. It takes time, and those minds sometimes need repeated exposure to the same idea for your business to solidify into a stable, long-lasting memory.

For most consultants, this process of building up the hundreds or thousands of memories that underlie a reputation/market position takes years. In years one and two of this process, you have some latitude to experiment with how you've specialized. Those early experiments and tweaks to your specialization don't threaten to undo years of reputation/market position-building work that you've done because . . . you haven't been doing that work for years yet.

Specialization never precludes making changes to your business. In fact, specialization generally leads to more power or profitability in your business, and that means

"How much is enough," you ask? That's an unanswerable question; you just know when it happens because you *feel it*, and it tends to happen faster than you think it will after you decide to specialize and start implementing the decision.

This longer timeline is one of the big differences between specialization/ positioning in the context of a small services business and positioning a commodity-like service or product. Products often use scaled impersonal outreach (paid advertising) to quickly establish their reputation/ position within the minds of the market, and often require a much larger market in order to succeed.

you can make future changes from a position of greater strength.

Specialization is not a face tattoo where if the tattoo artist is having a bad day, you get to live with that for the rest of your life. Later on, after you have built up the asset of a good market position, you will naturally be more thoughtful and reserved about making changes, but early on in the process, you have a lot of latitude to experiment and see how the market responds.

Beachheads Are Not Monastic Vows

I once spent a weekend at the Abbey of Gethsemani near Bardstown, Kentucky where Thomas Merton was a member for 27 years, but I don't really know what it's like to live as a monk.

I do know that many fear that specializing will be like taking the vows of a monastic order and that it will be a life of profound renunciation and monotony. If this person is an employee, there is a small chance they are right. If this person is self-employed, there is a 99 percent chance they are wrong.

If ever an actual monk reads this book, let me assure you I believe that monastic life is very rich and rewarding for those who practice it. I'm using the popular view of it as a convenient example rather than actually commenting on actual monastic life, which again, I don't have firsthand knowledge of.

Specializing is not a commitment to monotony. It is, to an extent, a repudiation of chasing shiny objects and unprofitable distractions, but it is not a commitment to boredom.

I'll elaborate on this in Section 2, but for now, I'll just claim that specialization is more interesting than operating as a generalist. It is not a monastery for business owners with face tattoos.

The Basics of Choosing a Beachhead

Specialization helps you earn visibility. Choosing a beachhead helps you build up the access and momentum needed to successfully specialize. So how do you choose a beachhead?

There are many reasons you might choose a particular beachhead:

- What's going to produce results quickly?
- What's going to get you to the place you want to be long-term?
    - Maybe that's defined in terms of impact
    - Maybe that's defined in terms of what lets you be of service to those you care about
    - Maybe you seek fame
    - Maybe you seek self-cultivation or personal transformation through your work
- What's going to avoid overwhelming you with a visibility-earning learning curve you're not ready for?

- What's going to be an enjoyable-enough specialization for you?

- What's going to be a lucrative specialization for you?

- What's going to be a low-risk, long-lasting specialization that lets you settle into simply doing the work you want to do?

There are more reasons, but those are the most common ones.

If your view is that an indie consulting business is a way to make the most amount of income you can while working for yourself, then you'll choose your specialization beachhead on that basis. And I'll celebrate that. If you view your business as a way to get the maximum enjoyment from your working hours, then that will influence how you choose a beachhead. And I'll celebrate that too.

One of the gifts of working as an independent consultant is freedom from the kind of structure and control found in other professions. The price is working harder to earn visibility, but once we've paid the fare for this particular trip, why not enjoy it?

Why not choose a beachhead based on what gives you some access and momentum that you can build on to create the kind of business *you* want?

Chapter 7: Two Forms of Risk That Threaten Successful Specialization

Specializing gives you leverage in earning visibility, but it also incurs risk. For example, vertical specialization is the easier way of focusing, but some verticals are inhospitable to outsiders. The uncertainty of whether you will be perceived as an outsider or not creates risk. That's one of the forms of risk involved in specializing.

The other is using the wrong decision-making heuristic.

When you decide how you want to specialize, you are making a tradeoff. Short-term revenue versus long-term opportunity, enjoyment versus profit, that kind of thing. Specialized indie consultants can get most of what they want out of this tradeoff, but getting *everything* you want *all the time* is unrealistic.

There are three patterns I've seen when people make the set of tradeoffs involved in specializing.

The first is when someone chooses a specialization based on what will quickly and efficiently lead to traction in the market. This is their **"head start."** They identify where they have the best head start, and build their specialization around the relative advantage their head start offers. This is the lowest-risk way to specialize. It is the safest beachhead to land on.

The second approach is when someone chooses a specialization based on **what kind of people** they want to work with. This may sound like a casual or strange way to make this kind of decision, but it's actually quite common. This way of deciding seems to be trading opportunity to gain enjoyment, and I'm sure in some cases it is, but if you believe as I do that consulting is ultimately about helping people respond to or initiate change, then deciding to focus on helping people that you *like and enjoy working with* can lead to greater *effectiveness* in your work which can lead to greater *impact* which can lead to more *opportunity* (revenue, profit, etc.). There are plenty of examples of optimizing both enjoyment and opportunity.

The third and final way of choosing a specialization is to pursue an **entrepreneurial thesis**. Instead of looking for what kind of clients you prefer to serve or what problems you find most fascinating and compelling, you are looking for the opportunity that seems like the best bridge from your current position to a significant entrepreneurial opportunity. In situations where people use the entrepreneurial thesis decision-making approach, the *potential business upside of the opportunity* is the most important factor in how they decide to specialize, and factors like enjoyment of the people or enjoyment of the work are much less important.

I've described these three ways of deciding on a specialization in order of increasing riskiness. When I wrote above that "the other form of risk is using the wrong decision-making heuristic," I really mean that taking on *excessive risk* is problematic, risk can come from the specialization itself, and it can come from how you decide on the specialization.

Risk Has Two Primary Components

Risk is the potential for harm that can result from uncertainty or volatility. A large amount of uncertainty does not lead directly to a high potential for harm. If I went to a restaurant where I love every item on the menu (there are a few like that for me here in Taos, NM) and asked the waiter to bring me whatever they feel like, there is a large amount of uncertainty and *no potential for harm*. I'm going to enjoy the heck out of a delicious meal no matter what they bring to the table. Lots of uncertainty, but no real risk.

Risk = Uncertainty x Potential for Harm

Many folks fear specializing. What they actually fear is the uncertainty surrounding the whole thing, but they visualize and react to the potential for harm part of the risk of specializing. They visualize:

- A repetitive, boring work life

- A deadly reduction in opportunity

- Screwing their business up by operating far outside their comfort zone

When we get into this fear-heavy state of mind, many of us visualize a maximized form of potential harm rather than a more realistic range of potential harm. The more realistic range looks like this:

- You work harder than you're used to for six to twelve months while you reorient your marketing around your new specialization.

- You make a suboptimal specialization choice the first time, spend a frustrating six months working at it, then pivot to something better (using the insight gained from those frustrating first six months) and find traction in the new focus.

- Your new specialization approach has you pursuing better but more demanding clients and you lose the first three sales opportunities, but your win rate increases sharply after that.

When evaluating risk, you must evaluate the potential for harm apart from the uncertainty because we are biased to assume that a large amount of uncertainty is directly correlated with a large potential for harm. We visualize risk-taking like a game of Russian roulette with the revolver having 30 chambers and one bullet — lots of uncertainty combined with extreme potential for harm. That is sometimes the case, but not always. When you look at the game of specializing, the potential for harm is almost always lower than you believe it is.

You should avoid taking on excessive risk when you specialize. This is not because the excessive risk will ruin you. It probably won't, in fact, because the potential for harm when specializing is quite low. But no matter how many times I write "high uncertainty is not the same as high potential for harm", we're all biased to believe the opposite.

The real danger with specializing is *flinching*.

The Role of Flinching in Specialization

Source: *Cambridge Dictionary*

Flinch: to make a sudden small movement because of pain or fear.

Business decisions—like the decision to specialize—are often compared to bets in a game of chance. While there are some similarities, especially when it comes to preparing to make a bet, business decisions are fundamentally different from bets because business decisions turn into results *when we implement them over time*.

Bets are resolved by the unalterable game mechanics of a spinning roulette wheel or a sports team's performance; our business decisions are resolved by *the operational performance of the same people who made the decision*. Us. We decide and then we implement. We are the gambler *and* the roulette wheel.

Along the way, we face numerous opportunities to undermine our own decisions. Maybe we want to move upmarket, but we hold back from opportunities to build new visibility in that upmarket segment— perhaps by giving talks or reaching out to podcast

63

hosts—because of the emotional or financial cost of the needed investment. Because of fear. The decision we made was fine, but it was undermined by a flimsy implementation of the decision.

This is flinching. Flinching is undermining your specialization decision by hastily responding to fear. This is the reason why you should not grossly exceed your risk profile when specializing, and this is why it's important to have a clear-eyed understanding of the benefits and risks involved in various ways of specializing.

If you understand the risks and tradeoffs involved in various ways of specializing, you'll be less prone to flinch as you implement the decision.

Chapter 8: Tradeoffs in the Five Ways of Specializing

If you want to use specialization to enhance your ability to earn visibility, you'll need to choose a specialization approach.

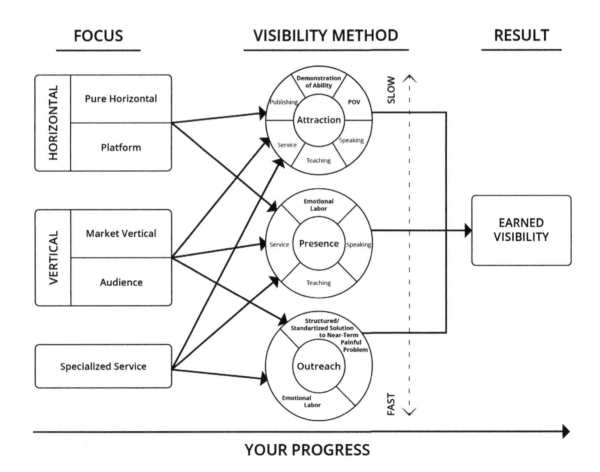

You might find that one of the five specialization approaches is an obvious fit for your business. If so, great! Go with it. Don't waste any more time doing book learning, because you need to start learning by doing. Motion generates information, and I'm not talking about the motion of flipping pages in this book.

If the idea of specializing still feels risky, then heed that gut feeling and explore the tradeoffs that each specialization approach poses.

You already know about the core risks of a platform specialization; the platform ecosystem will commoditize faster than you can evolve from an innovation business to an efficient business, or you won't want to make that shift so the platform ecosystem will become inhospitable to your innovation business.

Let's look at the benefits and risks of vertical and horizontal specialization.

Vertical Specialization Benefits

It's relatively easy. Check out the LinkedIn advanced search feature. The list of industries there doesn't map perfectly to the NAICS list I linked you to earlier, but it's close enough to make finding prospective buyers pretty trivial, at least for a pure vertical focus.

This makes earning visibility through outbound methods easier as well. Your marketing message is also probably easier to figure out. A typical example will be moving from describing your business using language like "elegant solutions to complex problems" to something like "custom software for retail financial services".

Word of mouth tends to spread most readily in a vertical fashion. It's kind of obvious, but I'll say it anyway: people in the same industry tend to interact with others in . . . the same industry. From conferences to industry publications to asking a colleague at a different company for a recommendation, word of mouth spreads most readily in a vertical fashion.

You've probably heard of "not invented here" syndrome. This tends to exist most heavily at the boundary between really different verticals. If you work in the finance industry and need to solve a high-speed trading problem, would you ask for a consultant recommendation from a colleague who works in the food and beverage industry? Probably not.

Past clients who leave their employer are most likely to land at a new employer in the same vertical. They can take you with them or at least open doors for you at their new employer. This helps you "stack" related experience more readily.

It's unsexy and downright unappealing to lots of creative types. If you're not put off by the unsexiness of it, that very unsexiness is a barrier to competition, but on the flip side, you might just not be able to imagine how focusing on a single vertical could possibly lead to an interesting career. You're probably wrong, but I get it.

I distinguish between so-called Creatives, which generally refers to designers, copywriters, etc., and the broader way in which consultants use creativity to solve problems. I think of readers of this book as creative people, even if you don't identify as a so-called Creative.

67

On its surface, it does seem like a limiting choice, but if you've never gone beyond a surface level of expertise, I can understand how you'd have trouble seeing the richness that lies beneath. It's like seeing a small, plain-looking mouth of a cave and not knowing that what actually lies beyond the mouth of the cave is a fascinating, complex system of caverns, sparkling with jewel-like mineral formations. Most vertical specializations will be just as interesting if you go deep enough.

It can be easier to forge strategic partnerships with other firms practicing different disciplines (marketing, accounting, law, etc.) specialized in the same vertical, super-connectors within the vertical (podcasters, associations, conference organizers, etc.), and product vendors like specialized SaaSes, etc.

It shortens the growth path from skill to expertise and from implementor to advisor. By serving a group of businesses that have a lot in common, you will find more opportunity and incentive to become conversant in what's important to the business, allowing you to quickly learn how to create real impact in the context of that vertical.

Vertical Specialization Risks

Not every vertical is equally receptive to outsiders. If you're truly an outsider to a vertical, trying to specialize in that vertical is a risk you should measure carefully.

Verticals can suffer business downturns that are localized to that vertical. 2007 would have been a pretty bad year for anyone to specialize in the real estate, mortgage, or construction verticals. The economic pain that ramped up in 2008 was more widespread than just those verticals, but they certainly were ground zero for a lot of economic carnage, and a service provider unlucky enough to get excited about specialization and then decide to specialize in serving one of *those* verticals at that time would have been in for a rough ride.

Vertical specialization ultimately requires you care about financial results, people, or business as much or more than you care about your technical skill set. For some folks, this will be no problem. In fact, it will increase enjoyment of their work. The ability to converse intelligently with their clients about the personalities, power dynamics, relationships, and culture of their business along with industry trends and the specifics of competitors is a powerful way for these folks to deepen the impact their technical skills create, and they'll love every minute of this advisor-level role.

However, others will find these exact same things a distracting nuisance and would rather focus on pure technical depth rather than acquire deeper knowledge of their client's business. These folks should probably avoid vertical specialization in favor of something horizontal in nature.

It is possible—though very unlikely—that if you pursue a vertical specialization, you will find client-side concerns about conflicts of interest (CoI). I can count on one hand the number of vertically specialized clients I've worked with who have *actually* had CoI concerns raised by their prospects.

If you do have a prospective client voice this concern, there's an 80 percent chance it's actually a late-stage sales objection or an attempt to prevent buyer's remorse. Their mindset has moved from excited to cautious, and they're now playing devil's advocate and trying to de-risk an opportunity they were previously excited about. As they do, they'll turn over every rock and leaf looking for a reason the proposed engagement might be a bad idea. A baseless CoI concern might surface, but if you're prepared for it, you can most likely defuse it.

A good resource on the late-sale flip from excited to cautious is this article from Blair Enns: www.winwithoutpitching.com/reassuring-words/

There's a very small chance that CoI is a real issue. Bigger organizations can internally firewall teams to prevent this, but as a soloist or very small company, it's often not possible to do this firewalling, so you may have to just walk away from opportunities where there is a genuine CoI concern. In reality, however, these situations are uncommon.

Horizontal Specialization Benefits

It's more naturally compatible with how consultants think. If you think in terms of process, frameworks, or any form of abstraction, then horizontal specialization is more naturally compatible with how you think than vertical specialization. Horizontal specialization seems to promise a lot of flexibility in who you work for and where you get to apply your process or framework, and that matches how most consultants are used to thinking.

It's easier for the typical consultant to imagine how horizontal specialization will remain an interesting, deep challenge for them over time. While it's not actually *true* that horizontal is inherently more interesting than vertical, it *seems* to be true because of the aforementioned way that you are used to thinking about things. This lowers the emotional barriers for consultants to enter a horizontal market position.

There are so many *experiential* aspects to what it's like to be an in-demand specialist that it's hard to convince "unbelievers" that vertical specialization can be just as interesting as horizontal, but I promise you, it can. To be fair, it can be *if* it's compatible with your personality and where you want to take your career.

I'm not sure I can prove this, but I believe horizontal specialization (or a very narrow horizontal focus coupled with a somewhat broader vertical focus) is a **more suitable specialization model for the so-called "lone wolves,"** meaning solo consultants who have no desire to build a team or agency business. This is because the pure vertical focus generally deploys a broader discipline (i.e., marketing, management consulting, custom software development) to a specific vertical. The breadth of the discipline itself benefits from a team of people with a blend of capabilities.

Horizontal Specialization Risks

It can require more work, lead time/runway, and marketing sophistication to find clients. One of the most fundamental differences between vertical and horizontal specialization is the relative absence of external signals of buying intent from the latter. To illustrate this, let's compare how two different specialists might earn visibility trust with prospective clients:

1. Juliette specializes in marketing for franchises. This is a vertical focus; specifically, an audience focus. Her marketing can be as simple as reaching out to franchises (they're easy to find because their business model is clearly externally visible) and saying a version of this: "Hi! I have no idea if you have an expert in franchise marketing working with you already, but if you don't—or if your current agency doesn't understand franchises as well as you'd like—we should talk. I've been specializing in marketing for franchises for years now and I'm sure I could bring some fresh ideas and depth of experience to move the needle for you. Again, if you've already got this covered, I'm really happy to hear that and please excuse the interruption, but if you don't have this covered and want to talk, I'd be happy to connect."

Juliette will almost certainly invest in other forms of marketing like content marketing, speaking, and so on. But, if all she had was a list of email addresses for CMOs at 500 franchises and the email copy above, I'd bet real money on her landing a few exploratory sales conversations from that email list, that email message, and a bit of persistent, polite follow-up.

2. Mike specializes in infrastructure and application monitoring. This is a horizontal specialization; specifically, a pure horizontal specialization. He's not a platform specialist because he's not focused on a single tool; he's focused on the business problem of using monitoring to move some desirable needle-like application availability.

How does Mike connect and build trust with prospective clients? Let's imagine he uses Juliette's approach and cold emails CIOs with an approach similar to Juliette's. The reality is, he's going to get nowhere. What *does* work for him?

He told me as much in this interview: consultingpipelinepodc ast.com/121

Writing an O'Reilly Media book on his area of expertise, launching and editing a popular weekly email list on the subject of monitoring, and conference speaking have been far more effective lead generation approaches for Mike. This is what I mean when I say a horizontal specialization can require more patience and skill in marketing.

These are also all Attraction visibility methods.

You may be in for a longer sales cycle or an unpredictable/heterogeneous sales process. Horizontal specialists often (but not always) specialize in business problems that are somewhat idiosyncratic. That's what makes them opportunities! The client hasn't developed an internal capacity to handle the problem, few other service providers have the nose for opportunity and risk tolerance required to specialize in

73

this same way, and the problem is not a routine, ongoing thing your client wants to outsource.

If you're an agency selling marketing services, you can integrate with a somewhat standard process your client has for selecting and purchasing your services. But if you're like Mike, solving a problem in the above example, there's almost certainly no standardized process for working with a monitoring expert. As a result, the sales process is going to be much more improvised, at least on the client side. This can be good or bad. It's good if your buyer has the authority to say, "Just make this happen. I can authorize payment myself." You've just bypassed a normally time-consuming process and closed a deal with a few conversations. But if you have to crawl an opaque web of decision makers or are dealing with a buyer who can't just cut a check without higher-up approval, then it's problematic that there's no standard purchasing process. You have to feel your way through a dimly-lit landscape of stakeholders and approval, and that landscape might not look at all like the next client where you have to feel your way through a different landscape, adding time and effort (cost, really) to the sale.

This potentially more difficult, complex sales process can be worth it if the problem you solve is important and is urgently felt by your clients. I'm not arguing for or against horizontal specialization here, just trying to alert you to something that may become a fact of life if you specialize in this way.

It can be easy to confuse the *technical difficulty* of the solution with the *economic value* of the solution. This one is insidious, and leads to disappointing situations that seem like great ways of specializing that do actually lead to some increased visibility, but then lead to little business opportunity.

It's so easy for you to see how difficult some problems are to solve and conflate the *difficulty* of solving the problem with the *economic value* of solving that problem. It's also easy to evaluate the economic value of solving a problem from your perspective as an outsider and not from the perspective of a business.

Businesses do seemingly dumb stuff all the time. Some of it actually *is* dumb. After all, not all businesses succeed, and sometimes their lack of success is due to truly dumb decisions. But sometimes business do "dumb" things for smart reasons, and sometimes those "dumb" things lead to positive outcomes for the business.

Maybe they operate in a regulated environment and do stuff that's technically dumb (i.e., paper records instead of electronic) because of the demands of regulation, and the cost of regulatory risk or noncompliance is actually far higher than the cost of the "dumb" thing they're doing. A consultant at the superficial level of expertise sees this situation and thinks it's wasteful, inefficient, and shortsighted. A consultant operating from deeper expertise sees the same situation and understands the *context* that makes the "dumb" decision the *right* decision.

The antidote here is simple but not easy. Learn to see things from both your perspective *and* your client's perspective, and gain enough insight into their perspective that you can almost read their mind. If you can make use of their worldview almost as fluently as your own, you'll be able to understand what problems could make for an economically viable pure horizontal specialization.

There is a special case here, which usually takes the form of developing specialized horizontal expertise that very few businesses would pay consulting rates to access, but a lot of your *peers* will individually pay small but collectively significant amounts of money to access.

Here's a good example from the world of tech. Adrian Rosebrock teaches developers how to integrate computer vision into Python. This isn't the exact situation I describe above, but it's close because Adrian has chosen to focus his business on individual devs more than large companies. Even if few businesses would pay consulting rates to access Adrian's expertise, a lot of his peers pay an individually small—but collectively significant—amount of money for that access.

This model works because instead of trying to sell expertise that few businesses demand, you "aggregate" the market demand for that expertise coming from your peers and sell your expertise to them in the form of training, coaching, mentoring, etc. Doing this often gets you corporate clients anyway, but it's a second-order effect of being successful in selling training to

In the best scenario, you get paid twice; once for the training and then a second time in the form of credibility, access, or both to corporate buyers.

individuals who then become sort of like an unpaid sales team for you.

You're smart, so I trust you've seen that no form of specialization is risk-free, and none is an all-you-can-eat buffet of benefits. It's tradeoffs all the way down.

Section 2

How You Earn Trust

Chapter 9: We Are Average at Trust-Earning

Let's be honest with ourselves. We are utterly average at earning trust.

If we happen to be good at it, we need to ask if it is really because the bar is low and the thing we're good at earning trust for is not really that important in the grand scheme of things. After all, we do practice a profession in which the world does not insist on requiring a license or continuing education. Most of us earn around a 90th percentile income with far less formal training, certification, or licensing than is required of a dental hygienist (73rd percentile) or massage therapist (48th percentile).

Or maybe it's because consulting is new? The discipline of management consulting, if we use Wikipedia's history of it, is only 126 years old. Lawyers have been allowed to take fees for services for around 2,000 years. It seems to take a while to build up the infrastructure of a profession.

They've existed in an informal sense for longer than that!

Either way, the task of earning sufficient trust from our prospective clients is thrust upon us as individual indie consultants. There's no standards body to confer trust upon us through licensing, and most of us get started doing project work that can't imprison or kill anybody (or any organization), and so it's relatively easy for us to earn enough trust to do that kind of inconsequential-in-the-grand-scheme-of-things work.

And so we are average at earning trust, and this is *fine*. We trundle along doing good work and then one day we decide want to do *better* work. Work that actually is more impactful and would therefore require more trust from our prospects. Or work that would be genuinely transformative for them, if they could just trust us enough to embark on a journey of transformation together.

When we hit this trust-earning ceiling, we start to get more interested in understanding how trust is built. Let's start there.

Inherited Trust and Preternatural Trust Magic

Our first move when facing the "How do I earn trust?" question is to examine the landscape around us and observe what others are doing to earn trust. As we do this, we will first notice others who have inherited or lucked their way into trust, and then we will notice those who are earn trust but don't seem to have to work hard at it.

Back to Matt Cutts, the former Google employee who—if he had become an indie consultant after leaving Google—would have immediately become the single most visible consultant in the SEO world. He also

Yes, you can earn visibility without trust. Examples include Donald Trump and Vladimir Putin.

would have become the most *trusted* consultant in the SEO world.

This is inherited trust, and when we think about the idea of pedigree, we are thinking about inherited trust. Using *inherited* in the way I am here is intentional. It's not that Matt Cutts didn't work his ass off at Google and develop real, transferable expertise there. I'm sure he did. But if he'd put in the same hard work at Microsoft on their Bing search engine, he would inherit less trust because Bing is a second-tier, rather than first-tier, search engine. Matt Cutts is an example of inheriting trust from a parent institution.

Consultants who leave large, famous consulting firms inherit trust from their old employers. Employees who leave a management position at a company to become self-employed inherit trust from their old employers as well. In these cases, the market trusts that if the consultant's expertise was valuable enough for Google or McKinsey, for example, it's good enough for the market.

There are others who, though lacking pedigree, have a preternatural ability to earn trust from strangers. Maybe they are exceptionally good bullshitters, or maybe they are simply exceptionally good with people. These people's trust-earning ability is truly horizontal; they could earn enough trust to sell waterfront luxury condos in Miami, tractors in North Dakota, or consulting services in Silicon Valley.

Most of us, though, have a mediocre ability to earn trust. We lack that preternatural trust magic, and we eventually reach a point where the opportunities we seek require more or a different type of trust than we're easily able to earn, and so we have to figure out how to earn deeper levels of trust. Our limited trust-earning ability starts to create a ceiling on our business's ability to access opportunity.

It's at this point we start to care about the other part of "doing marketing," which is earning trust.

Chapter 10: Methods of Earning Trust

If you're like me, you look at those with inherited trust-earning ability and feel a mixture of envy and pity. Envy, for the advantage they now possess, but pity for the years they spent working for a boss in order to get it. You look at those with preternatural trust-earning ability and mutter "Freaks!" under your breath.

And then, you keep scanning the landscape to find examples of those who earn trust in a way that's compatible with your lack of pedigree and lack of magical trust-earning ability. That's when you notice the . . . what to call these folks? They have experimented and worked and found *something* that helps them exceed their natural supply of God-given trust-building ability. In craftsman-like fashion, they've learned how to earn deeper levels of trust and become sufficiently competent at it. Let's call them the journeymen of trust-earning.

The Journeymen of Trust-Earning

This group contains four subgroups: the insider, the articulate craftsman, the mountain climbing guide, and the visionary. All of these subgroups have gotten reasonably good at *something* that earns deeper trust, either as a direct outcome or as a second-order consequence.

The insiders are transferred trust when given as a referral, or they use various forms of *affinity* to earn trust.

With insiders, the buyer has decided to buy something specific and is evaluating options and finds that greater levels of affinity produce a warm, trust-y, like-y feeling. These affinities might include:

- Shared experience(s)/background

- Shared social group membership

- Shared jargon

- Shared culture

- Shared worldview

- Shared social status

- Shared enemies

- Shared authorities

Some affinities can't be predicted or created, they just happen. If you and a prospective client went to the same university, that might create a feeling of affinity and lead to some of that warm, trust-y, like-y feeling that affinity often creates. But you can't engineer this form of affinity for every possible prospect; it would be a massive overinvestment in university tuition and time!

Other forms of affinity can be engineered by learning your buyers jargon, culture, worldview, and so on. You can make yourself an insider—at least partially—to your prospects' world through curiosity, empathy, and work. You also can't engineer this form of affinity for every possible prospect, but if you focus on a narrow range of prospects, you can become an insider and thereby earn deeper trust.

With **the articulate craftsmen**, the buyer is suffering a problem, the consultant is offering a matching solution, and the consultant explains the mechanics of the solution well enough that the buyer feels that they can trust the solution, and thereby comes to trust the purveyor of the solution: you.

The articulate craftsman's ability to earn trust will be highest when the fit is good between the client's problem and the consultant's solution. In fact, their ability to earn deeper trust flows from how good the problem–solution fit is. This means that if the consultant wants to earn trust from a lot of people, they need to engineer a solution that fits a lot of those people's business problems right out of the box, with little or no modification. They need to engineer a consulting solution that looks like a product, and sell it using the kind of process you would with a product.

Alternately, the articulate craftsman can engineer a solution that fits just a few people's business problems and, if the underlying value is there, charge a lot for the solution. The articulate craftsman may end up being trusted by a few people, or by many.

With **the (mountain climbing) guide**, the buyer understands the journey they want to undertake ("I want to climb Mount Everest") but doesn't know the particulars of the journey (left versus right turns, which crevasses are actually dangerous versus merely scary looking). The buyer needs a guide. The consultant demonstrates expertise about this particular journey, and in so doing, earn the trust of an informed buyer.

The guide and the articulate craftsman differ in the scope of their work. The craftsman is building a solution that sticks closely to a pattern, while the guide is helping their client navigate a journey that encompasses more unknowns that have to be figured out on the fly (sudden storms, rockslides, etc.). The craftsman just needs to demonstrate the appropriate fit for the solution to earn sufficient trust. The problem and solution both operate in a domain with relatively few unknowns.

The guide operates in a domain with many more unknowns, and their trust-earning task reflects this. It is the task of describing past successes *and* the thinking and problem-solving method that made those journeys successful. It is the task of conveying both accomplishment and flexibility in the face of future unknowns.

Finally, **the visionary** helps prospects decide whether they want to be mountain climbers at all. They address those who have never climbed mountains or only climbed smaller mountains, and help them imagine what that accomplishment would look, feel, smell, and taste like. The visionary may also guide recruits on

their climb, or hand those recruits off to someone else
for guidance along the actual journey.

The visionary may actually know relatively little about
the particular turns and dangers of the trip up the
mountain. They may know a lot more about the
dissatisfactions and limitations of non-mountain
climbing life, and their desire is focused on simply
seeing more people give mountain climbing a try. In
less metaphorical terms, they might be focused on
seeing general improvement in the market they're
focused on. If we could hear their internal dialog, we
might hear: "I wish these people would aspire to *more*!"

There is something about how these visionaries are able
to talk about the accomplishment or transformation
that comes about from the journey that earns trust from
a sliver of the market. Maybe some prospects were
feeling a vague itch to change and the visionary helps
them settle on mountain climbing instead of deep sea
diving. Maybe some prospects had decided that next
year is the year they're going to finally climb a friggin'
mountain, and the visionary helps them decide on
which mountain to climb. And maybe some prospects
feel generally stuck, and the visionary convinces them
that mountain climbing is the best way to get unstuck.

When done in a compelling fashion, the expression of
vision both creates (or amplifies) the desire for change
and earns the trust needed to facilitate the change.

The insider, the articulate craftsman, the mountain
climbing guide, and the visionary are the subgroups we
see when we look at the journeymen of trust-earning

who have learned how to earn deeper levels of trust and become sufficiently competent at it. The insiders and articulate craftsmen have the easiest trust-earning task; the guides and visionaries have the most difficult task because theirs is the work of *leadership*.

Chapter 11: The Relationship Between Specialization and Trust

The journeymen of trust-earning have specialized. They have done this because becoming an insider, an articulate craftsman, a guide, or a visionary *requires* specialization.

How You Can Be Average and Trustworthy

As we continue to examine the landscape around us and observe what others are doing to earn trust, we notice that some consultants seem to lack extreme smarts and pedigree, but have an easy time earning trust from buyers because they "speak the buyer's language" or are quickly able to socialize in a beyond-the-surface-level way. These folks bring an average level of expertise to the conversation, but an above-average ability to earn trust.

These folks have often specialized vertically.

By choosing one market vertical to focus on or one pseudo vertical like e-commerce, they have made themselves insiders to their prospect's and client's

E-commerce is a pseudo vertical because, while it is actually distributed across many verticals, its market dynamics (watering holes, sense of identity, etc.) are similar to that of a true vertical.

world. They know their prospect's language and jargon. They know what kind of changes are going to hurt and which are merely business as usual. They know how the money gets made and how it gets spent. And they understand who generally has hard power, who has soft power, and who has both. If they were challenged to define a "Maslow's hierarchy of needs" for the vertical they are focused on, they could do it easily.

A deep understanding of the needs, problems, aspirations, constraints, and opportunities facing a market is *market insight*. Market insight is really what helps vertical specialists earn deeper trust.

Some of these average-expertise-but-above-average-at-trust-earning consultants seem to "engineer" referrals (and the trust those confer) by cultivating relationships with complementary service providers. Those complementary service providers might be in the same vertical or in the same horizontal market. The "engineering" of the relationship isn't nefarious or mercenary, it's simply building intentional business relationships.

Example: A bank refers clients who have a difficult land use approval process ahead of them to a PR consultant who specializes in difficult land use approvals.

Example: A business strategy consultant refers prospects who want to sell a business to an M&A specialist.

How Appropriate Fit Earns Trust

Some of these average-expertise-but-above-average-at-trust-earning consultants seem to earn trust while they are clearly explaining how precisely their standardized solution fits a prospect's problem. It's not that the consultant is great at earning trust; it's more that their solution feels trustworthy because of how well engineered it is to solve the need or problem the prospective client has.

We see this form of trust-building most often with those who have specialized one or more of their services, even if their business as a whole is not specialized vertically or horizontally. The sales process for the specialized service is usually developed in a way that creates a feeling of safety for prospects, and this feeling of safety—along with the aforementioned appropriate fit—is what earns trust.

How Narrow Mastery Earns Trust

And finally, we see some consultants who seem incredibly smart about a specific topic and seem to get buyers' heads nodding along very quickly in a conversation.

In reality, they may not be all that impressive in terms of intelligence or life choices, but when in a conversation with prospective clients, they are able to quickly focus on what's important and problematic to the prospect, and from that conversational beachhead, they are able to build a lot of trust quickly.

We notice this form of trust-earning skill when we are observing those who have specialized for a while—at least two to three years.

Partial Truths Earlier in This Book

I told you some partial truths earlier. I did this to incrementally build up a model without the burden of excessive complexity, not to deceive you.

For example, I said "Specialization is a lever to help you get more out of your investment in visibility." That is partially true. Specialization is also a lever to help you build trust.

Really, specialization is a lever to help you get more out of your investment in visibility *and* augment your ability to earn trust from prospects.

Chapter 12: The Market Power of Leadership and Management

You might trust both Bill Gates and the person who babysat you as a kid to babysit *your* child, but you'd probably only trust one of those people to be on the board of directors of a large business. Not all forms of trust are equal. It's obvious that there are differences in *quantity* when it comes to trust, but there are also differences in *quality*.

Let's visualize a spectrum that runs from *leadership* to *management* on the other. This spectrum differentiates various types of leadership and the *market power* of the trust flowing from those forms of leadership. It looks

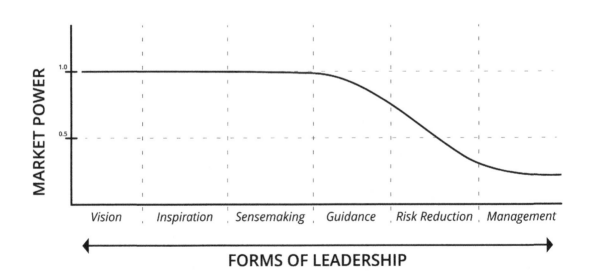

The styles of leadership on the left end of this spectrum generate more valuable forms of trust. They're more valuable because they're more closely connected to advisory work, keynote speaking slots, and services that leverage your time more profitably. And they're more valuable because they're scarcer.

Management, on the other hand, is less valuable because it is more common and more understood. Every truly good manager is a gift to the human race and we'd be screwed without y'all, but there are simply more of you good managers than there are people who can use a stage, YouTube channel, email list, or even a one-to-one conversation to build a vision for something new, risky, and worthwhile. Management is a form of leadership, but when I talk about leadership in the context of trust-building for the rest of this book, I'm only talking about building vision, inspiring action, making sense of change, providing guidance, and reducing risk. These are the leadership styles that have the greatest power in the marketplace.

Building a Leadership Position

The warm, trust-y feeling between a lot of people and you—the feeling that enables the role of leader or authority—doesn't happen overnight. It takes time to build up a leadership position.

That means we need to think about how the systems within which we might want a leadership position change over time so that we don't build up leadership in the wrong place or the wrong context.

To think this through, we need to understand two things—commoditization and open/closed systems.

Commoditization Is the Reduction of Waste

Over time, things that society needs at scale (electricity, railroad tracks, project management methodology, design frameworks, etc.) move from innovation—where novelty and relative chaos prevail, to standardization—where utility and relative order prevail.

An innovation is an idea, practice, or object that is perceived as new and provides perceived relative advantage.

The early stage of an innovation's existence is defined by waste. When the innovation enters the market, it is poorly understood, and the innovation itself is relatively unreliable and un-standardized. This means that a few customers who have no business buying the innovation buy it anyway, and others who are better equipped to benefit from the innovation spend lavishly on understanding, customizing, implementing, fixing, and supporting it. From the perspective of those who embrace innovation early on, these are all normal forms of risk and overhead costs required to unlock the value (relative advantage) of the innovation.

From the future perspective, where the innovation has become fully commoditized, these are all forms of *waste*. They threaten the widest possible adoption of the innovation, so they must be reduced or eliminated.

As both the supply and demand sides of the market learn how to reduce the waste involved in producing, distributing, and consuming the innovation, prices inevitably move downward. Hungry suppliers use lower prices as a path toward greater market share, and the demand side of the market is always happy to normalize and insist on a lower price as long as it does not threaten the quality, consistency, and availability of the thing they are seeking.

And so as time marches on, if society needs the innovation at scale, it matures into a commodity. When the thing is new, we don't know if society will need it at scale because it's new! But we do know that if society ends up needing it at scale, it will commoditize.

Even in commodity markets, bespoke and luxury options still exist. Society wants automobiles at scale, yet there are still companies selling hand-built cars at a dramatically higher price point. But these hand-built cars represent a tiny share of the total automobile trade.

Closed Systems Are Like Ponds; Open Systems Are Like Rivers

From their early formative status, innovations march toward their final mature form as a commodity inside of some kind of *system*. Let's intentionally oversimplify all the systems out there into two kinds: open and closed systems.

Open systems, or complex systems, have no central control. They aren't owned and controlled by a central entity. There might be ownership, but it's distributed, not centralized, and the ownership is relative and negotiated, not absolute. Complex systems feature nonlinearity, which means the same cause can produce wildly different effects depending on what's happening inside the system. And finally, complex systems feature emergent behaviors, meaning the system interacts with its environment in complex ways.

The defining feature of closed systems is control, specifically some kind of *centralized control*. That control is expressed through ownership and control over the borders of the system.

Nonlinearity is the bane of business advice that's based on one-size-fits-all declarations or modeling prior successes in the hope of creating a precise recipe for success in the future.

The Relationship Between Openness, Leadership, and Management

Innovation often imposes change on a system. This is exogenous change. Leadership is helping a group respond to exogenous change or generate endogenous change; management is helping a group optimize the status quo.

Remember that when innovation enters a system, it is poorly understood, and the innovation itself is relatively unreliable and un-standardized. How much of your work is helping clients respond to those kinds of challenges—lack of know-how in applying not-yet-totally-figured-out technology or ideas? I'd wager that a *lot* of it is. As innovations mature and become understood and standardized (commoditized), clients need less help figuring out how to apply the technology or idea. They may need help managing it, but they usually have that capacity in-house.

Exogenous change and innovation are the oxygen that sustain the kind of leadership we indie consultants provide. Without change and innovation flowing into the system in which they operate, our clients need less leadership; mostly, they just need *good management*.

Open systems need more leadership than closed systems. They might need more management as well, but in terms of the ratio of leadership to management over the time span of decades, open systems need more leadership.

The Relationship Between Closedness, Leadership, and Management

Platforms are the *most* closed systems, both because of the control the platform owner wants (and probably needs) to assert, and because their ownership is concentrated rather than distributed. Small, isolated technology platforms are going to have the least innovation flowing through the platform itself, so leadership in this context is going to look more like the competence-based forms of leadership (e.g., risk reduction) rather than the more inspirational forms (vision building).

The problem? Young platforms pose this nearly irresistible offer: "Focus on me, become an expert in my ways, and I will reward you with overnight authority! Those who are hungry for knowledge about how to respond to the change I represent will flock to you and will see you as a demigod." Stacy, described in Chapter 3, took this deal.

If you get in early with the platform and start doing that vision/inspiration kind of leadership, the platform eventually won't need this kind of leadership if it matures into a relatively small, closed system. In this case, the value your leadership provides will erode as the platform evolves toward commodity status, needs less leadership, and more management. If the platform takes a different trajectory and becomes large and more relatively open, you won't face this problem, but *in the early days of the platform's life, you don't know how its evolution will unfold*, so platforms pose a dilemma. They really can help you become an overnight authority with all the trust-earning benefits that entails, but the ideal time to start focusing on the platform is early on in its evolution, and that is the point of maximum uncertainty about whether the platform will evolve into a closed system with the resulting declining value of leadership, or into a more open system that preserves the value of your leadership.

Vertical markets are less-closed systems. Vertical markets see multiple innovations pass through the domain of the market, so there is an ongoing, recurring opportunity for genuine leadership, especially through *sensemaking*—helping the market make sense of the latest innovation and make better decisions about how to respond to these waves of invaders. There are other trust-building opportunities as well, but you have to keep your allegiance with the market, not with the innovations that pass through the market.

And finally, there are *really* open, really large systems, which include broad horizontal topics (sales, marketing, employee performance, etc.) and, to an extent, huge relatively open platforms (Amazon's AWS is a good example). These systems are defined by a massive amount of *flow*, and the dynamism and chaos of that flow opens up all sorts of opportunities to lead and create value (and earn trust) by leading.

These large open systems also receive a constant inflow of newcomers, and the variety of needs those newcomers have ensures that no matter where you are focused in terms of leadership (vision versus risk reduction), you'll have a steady flow of newcomers who are seeking *your* style of leadership. The openness and ownerless nature of these systems means there's a constant inflow of uncontrolled novelty, and folks often look to their leaders/authorities for guidance on how to respond to these exogenous change curveballs.

There are long-lived leadership opportunities everywhere—except for platforms. When the platform is new, the leadership opportunities are there, and it's unnaturally easy to lay hold of these opportunities. The hidden cost of that ease is you really don't know whether the platform will become huge and stay relatively open like AWS, which is to say that you don't know whether your easily obtained leadership position will turn into a durable asset or will fade away like so many others have.

Anyone who says they knew in 2006 for sure how AWS was going to evolve and how important it was going to become is bullshitting.

To be clear, you can build a decent business within the system created by a platform, even if the platform ultimately evolves into a small, relatively closed system. You just have to be okay with evolving from a figure-shit-out innovation model to an efficient-and-consistent services delivery model, and that's not an easy or natural evolution for most indie consultants. That's why using a focus on a platform as a trust-earning lever is a risky decision.

The value of leadership positions in vertical markets
and horizontal markets are roughly equal. I don't think
there's a strategic reason to choose one over the other;
it's more a question of the three specialization decision-
making heuristics I mentioned in Chapter 8 leading
your specialization decision-making, and then doing
the best trust-earning work you can in the wake of the
specialization decision you made.

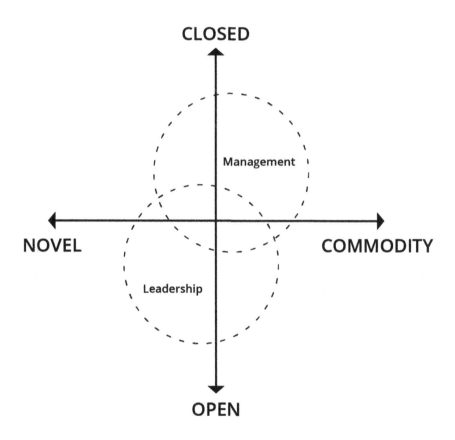

This stuff matters because we are not playing a short
game, and some of us are willing to walk through the
red-light district—teeming with young platforms

offering a quick trust-earning thrill—toward more open systems where we can build something both valuable and durable; something that allows us to earn trust through the rarer forms of leadership within a system that afford us ongoing opportunities to use and further refine those leadership skills. Something we love coming home to at night over decades and decades.

Chapter 13: A Model for Earning Trust

We now have enough observation to put together a model of how trust-earning works.

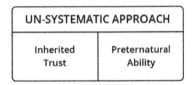

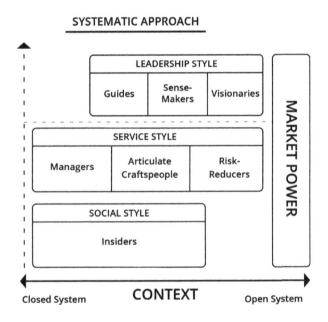

Inheriting trust or possessing preternatural ability are nice. They are also unsystematic approaches that can't be replicated by normal people—us.

We "normals" have access to three systematic approaches—things we can decide to do, learn to do, and implement with a normal allocation of skill and resources.

We can use social connections to earn trust. We can be of service. Or we can lead.

The Social Styles of Trust-Earning

You'll remember that earlier I referenced several forms of *affinity* that help some consultants become an insider to their clients' world:

- Shared experience(s)/background

- Shared social group membership

- Shared jargon

- Shared culture

- Shared worldview

- Shared social status

- Shared enemies

- Shared authorities

These are all primarily *social* styles of trust-earning. You'll also notice in our model that social styles have the least market power and, while they are effective across most of the spectrum, from closed to open systems, they are not effective in the most open of open systems.

George E. P. Box popularized this idea in the easily remembered form I've borrowed here.

This is a good place to remind you that all models are wrong, but good models are useful anyway. I think our model for trust-earning is a good model, but bear in mind that reality is more fuzzy and fluid than this model depicts. Precise, clear lines in the model are simplified representations of the fuzzy, permeable membranes of real life.

So when you see the box that represents the social styles of leadership extending only about 75 percent of the way toward the right end of the closed <—> open systems spectrum, I'm suggesting an observed norm, not an ironclad rule. The norm is this: in the most open of open systems, things are so chaotic and fast moving that the social relationships underpinning the social styles of trust-earning simply don't have time to form. In a fast-moving open system, everybody is a newcomer and everybody is, in a relative sense, a stranger to each other.

This doesn't mean that social styles of trust-earning are completely ineffective in the most open of open systems. Instead, it means the social styles are *relatively* less valuable; less useful for earning trust that you don't already have. This model is focused on how *context* (open versus closed systems) and *relative value* (market power) relate to various styles of trust-earning.

The Market Power versus the Actual Value of Trust

It's natural to see social styles of trust-earning as an easy, beginner-friendly entry point to the world of systematic trust-earning, but it's more complex than that. I have a friend who runs a marketing agency. He makes more money than I do and has a more outwardly impressive business than I do. His website is nicer. On the other hand, I spend more time on stages delivering presentations where I'm trying to lead my market someplace new. I play the role of the visionary.

My friend earns trust primary through social styles. He rarely gets on a stage and does not play the role of the visionary. What gives? I'm engaging in a style of trust-earning that has more market power. Why is his business financially outperforming mine?

Context, baby! My friend is very good at using social trust-earning styles in a systematic way. He learns where his best prospects hang out, buys a ticket to those events, and then uses his naturally gregarious, extroverted personality to build trusting relationships with other attendees. I, in the exact same situation, would keep to myself and walk away from the event with almost no new useful relationships to nurture into clients. I'm an aloof introvert, and while I can use social trust-earning styles, I need a small group, intimate context in order to succeed at this style of trust-earning. Additionally, it is in every way easier for me to get on a

And I *have been* in the exact same situation with this friend multiple times.

110

stage and deliver a visionary talk than to sit in the audience and build relationships with other attendees.

My friend sells services that produce nearly immediate value for his clients; mine take time to produce value. His services fit into a well-defined genre that companies are used to purchasing; mine do not. And so my friend has created a system that produces exceptional revenue quickly; I am doing something more like cloud-seeding to produce exceptional revenue later.

The point of this story is to illustrate how my friend uses a style of trust-earning that has less market power than mine to produce more short-term revenue than I do. Maybe I will ultimately out-earn my friend. That remains to be seen. The point: market power is not immediately and directly correlated to the revenue potential of your business. Market power, in our trust-earning model, is connected to the notions of thought leadership or authority and should be noted that while these are sources of power, their pursuit also entails risk and their monetization may be more difficult.

Does my friend wish he could use trust-building styles that have more market power? Nope! He has built a business with a harmonious relationship between who it's focused on, what it does for them, and how it earns trust, and he's optimized that business for exceptional profitability. Given that context, why would he invest in a riskier trust-earning style?

The model for trust-earning I'm presenting here is not a map of a journey. You don't start at the bottom (social styles) and climb your way to the top (leadership). You will have personal reasons (your personality, comfort zone, etc.) for starting with—and possibly sticking with—a particular style of trust-earning. You may have strategic reasons for shifting that style. But you're very unlikely to use all styles at once or to climb from the bottom to the top of this range of styles.

The Service Styles of Trust-Earning

Being of service can earn trust, but in these cases, what we actually seem to be trusting is the competence and reliability that underpin that service. It's convenient, however, to group the managers, the articulate craftspeople, and the risk reducers together into the trust-earning style of *service*.

"Management is doing things right; leadership is doing the right things."
– Peter Drucker

I wonder if those who identify as managers feel like Drucker is insulting them somehow. I also wonder if they are relieved *not* to be burdened with figuring out the right thing to do. That's my oblique confession to not really knowing how managers think in a sufficiently detailed way. But like you, when I observe the landscape of trust-earning, I can see a place where being a good manager is a great way to earn trust from consulting prospects.

"The managers"—meaning the larger group of those who make sure things get done the right way, not just the smaller group of those who have the word *manager* in their job title—earn trust through their service. They do these sorts of things:

- Explain how to do specific tasks or projects in a way that works reasonably well. They use media like blog articles, YouTube videos, podcast guest appearances, and talks from a stage.

- Build up reusable or broadly applicable forms of best practice as the system they operate within commoditizes (moves from chaos to order).

- Create a feeling of safety by generally furthering the chaos -> order progression of the system they operate within.

The management style of trust-building thrives in closed systems because those systems generally feature the least amount of change and novelty, so our managers are able to articulate their process-based, detail-oriented expertise with the least amount of compromise and caveating, and so are able to apply that expertise with a higher probability of success.

We can think of the risk reducers as managers who are more comfortable and adept at operating within the more chaotic and fast-moving open systems. Instead of detailed, expensive-to-change process documents, for example, we see them using lean or agile methods to reduce the inevitable cost of change present in extremely open systems. Instead of sharing recipes, we see them sharing frameworks.

The articulate craftspeople are more doers than managers, but they still have at least a genuine respect for—if not a deep love for—the process and control needed to produce excellent results with consistency. Their personal sense of identity springs more from the beauty or functionality of the work or the craft than from the business system that surrounds it. They are articulate because they love talking about it, explaining it, laying bare the art and/or science of it, or championing an improved state of the art for it.

The far horizon of most articulate craftspeople's vision is the edges of their own craft. This limited focus is shared by others who earn trust through service. They are somewhat "tribal," and this limits their market power. Those who earn trust through service are unlikely to steer or change an entire market. As I hope I've demonstrated with the example of my marketing agency friend, limited market power does not translate to limited business success or earning power.

The Leadership Styles of Trust-Earning

Do you know how daunting it is as a writer—how fraught—to try to use the word *leadership* in a meaningful way? I'm not as concise as Peter Drucker. Repeating my definition: Leadership is helping a group respond to exogenous change or generate endogenous change; management is helping a group optimize the status quo.

The guides in our model are like hands-off managers, but their job is to help clients with a journey of transformation, not optimization. The buyer understands the journey they want to undertake ("I want to climb Mount Everest") but doesn't know the particulars of the journey (left versus right turns, which crevasses are actually dangerous versus merely scary looking). The buyer needs a guide. The consultant demonstrates expertise about this particular journey, and in so doing, they earn the trust of an informed buyer.

Sense-makers make sense of change. They help us think about change and they help us answer questions like:

- "Is this change a threat, an opportunity, or . . . ?"

- "How do we contextualize this change? Is it big, small, a curveball, or . . . ?"

- "What does it *mean* that this is happening?"

- "Why is this happening now and not later?"

These questions are milquetoast—almost inert—when expressed in the abstract way I have here, but they take on real urgency and import when they are about relevant, current events for a particular audience. This gives sense-makers (and guides and visionaries) market power; it gives these trust-earning styles the ability to steer a market.

Leaders use the tools of story, narrative, maps, frameworks, ubiquity, status, speaking, and manifestos. They may operate using extensive data, gut feel, or anything in between. They may leverage the status of a single prestigious keynote talk or the ubiquity of 30 podcast guest appearances all released within a few months. They may make skillful use of comfort or shock or anything in between. No matter what tool, method, or style they use, their role is to generate or help us respond to change.

Closed systems need relatively little actual leadership; that is why in our model, the leadership style extends only partially into the region of closed systems. If the closed system is a *platform*, then the platform owner leads, and everyone else is a user or a vendor. Genuine third-party leadership is a potential threat to the platform owner. If the closed system is a stagnant vertical, there is relatively little change that needs responding to.

You Are Not Locked into One Trust-Earning Style

Again, all models are wrong, but good models are useful anyway. I think this is a decent model, but bear in mind that reality is more fluid than this model depicts.

For example, the management trust-earning style can become a sort of micro-beachhead into leadership. You might earn trust from a small audience through your management expertise, and that existing trust might allow you to serve as sense-maker or guide for that audience—as a leader—in the face of change and novelty. You could think of this as a "battlefield promotion" from manager to leader.

This kind of fluidity is what the real world is like, and so the boxes in our model should always be seen more like fuzzy focal points rather than rigid boxes with impermeable boundaries.

The Importance of Beachheads in Earning Trust

Specialization is a lever to help you get more out of your investment in visibility *and* augment your ability to earn trust from prospects. Where does the trust-earning leverage come from?

Specialization is a force multiplier. The same amount of modest, journeyman-like trust-earning work applied to a smaller area—fewer people in a smaller, specialized market—produces better results.

Beachheads build momentum. When you experience that first win, that first move beyond your previous trust ceiling, you start to believe in and feel the possibilities that specialization unlocks. These early wins fortify you for the long haul. They help you keep building and investing because you have physical evidence that your investment can pay off. This leads to *consistent presence* with the market you're focused on, and this consistency helps you earn trust more effectively.

This is true if you feel that you *earned* those early wins. If they are the result of luck, they have the opposite effect; they make the long haul seem intolerably long, difficult, and unfair.

117

Critically, beachheads shorten learning curves. As independent consultants, we tend to start out business with above-average skill or expertise in a discipline or a craft. I don't know if you'll believe me when I say that no matter how much of an expert you are now, *there is a lot more expertise you can cultivate*. So much more.

If you know *how*, you can know why. If you know *what*, you can see beyond first-order relationships into second and third-order effects in the context of a system. You can understand the patterns that are common to these systems. You can augment gut feel or experience with data. You can move from competence to expertise to mastery.

And if you master one domain, you can scale that mastery into more profitable intellectual property, or you can move up the value chain within your domain.

There is always more expertise you can cultivate. Beachheads are essential to shortening the learning curve. Some of these learning curves look like gaining deeper insight into your market. And some look like deeper forms of the expertise that you are selling your market.

Deeper insight into your market makes you more effective at earning trust, no matter what your trust-earning style is. The social styles benefit from better understanding those they are connecting with, the service styles benefit from better understanding how to serve the market, and the leadership styles benefit from better understanding those they are leading.

You would be correct in this belief; even small-scale data collection can help prospects trust you enough to take a bigger risk with you than they would without that data. It can also help you earn more visibility.

Let's say you wanted to augment your expertise in using storytelling to help companies sell innovative products, which has until now been rooted in your own experience, with more objective data. You believe that this investment in acquiring data will help you earn new trust in the marketplace and lead to better, more impactful client work.

You work on formulating the question that will guide your data collection. Which of these questions is the better choice?

1. Does the intentional use of storytelling help companies sell innovative products?

2. What percentage of the companies that have moved from the Visionaries to the Leaders quadrant of Gartner's Magic Quadrant for Cloud Computing in the last five years have CMOs or CEOs that talk publicly about storytelling as a strategic tool?

The first formulation of your research question is too broadly scoped and will delay the experience of *traction*. The second one offers a beachhead. It will result in an incomplete answer, which could be frustrating, but you will gain access to something that's far more important than completeness; you will trade completeness for *momentum*. This is a good trade because that momentum will help you efficiently progress toward your ultimate goal of augmenting your expertise in using storytelling to help companies sell innovative products with more objective data. This is just one example of how a beachhead shortens the expertise–cultivation learning curve.

Expertise is especially critical when you are earning trust through the articulate craftsperson, risk reducer, and leadership styles. The faster you can cultivate expertise that genuinely deserves to be called insightful, the better for your trust-earning ability. In other words, the sooner you can land better, more impactful opportunities.

If you use social trust-earning styles, specialization helps you become "monogamous" with your market. That helps with trust-earning.

If you use service trust-earning styles—even if you don't pursue the deepest layers of expertise—specialization shortens the learning curve that lies between your current level of skill and a very high level of competence and consistency in your work. Truly excellent levels of competence and consistency help earn trust.

And if you use leadership styles to earn trust, specialization and "monogamy" make it unlikely you'll be perceived as a mercenary. You will be more able to embrace the risk of leadership because you'll *actually* care about those you're seeking to lead, and you'll be willing to speak uncomfortable truths in service of their success.

The social trust-earning styles function without the benefit of specialization better than the others. But they have the least market power and the least versatility across the entire spectrum from closed to open systems.

One of reasons you might choose a particular specialization is this heightened level of care, and even if that wasn't why you chose the specialization, you'll tend to develop a caring relationship with the market you've specialized in eventually. Yes, your market will occasionally annoy you, but your interest in their success will overwhelm those occasional annoyances.

All the other trust-earning styles benefit from the leverage that specialization offers. In the context of earning new trust from a market, specializing creates a beachhead that leads to gaining genuine insight into the market quicker, and cultivating genuine expertise with which to create value for the market and your business.

The insight and expertise that you cultivate as a result of specialization helps you earn trust more effectively.

Chapter 14: Apply the Trust-Earning Model

All models are wrong, but good models are useful anyway; the most useful models inform important decisions. What about our trust-earning model?

Almost every indie consultant I have encountered can make use of some form of service to earn trust. It's what's most natural to most of us because we tend to think of ourselves as intentional craftspeople and accidental businesspeople. Service is what we do.

Not all of us, however, are willing to take on the emotional labor involved in the social styles, and some don't have the stomach for the risk of the leadership styles. The following specialization approaches tend to *require* that you use a leadership style to earn sufficient trust.

Big missions: A colleague of mine, Jonathan Stark, is on a mission to rid the world of hourly billing. This is not a small task, and it is not short-term work. Jonathan will never complete this mission, and I think he knows that and is fine with a mission that is what James Carse would call an infinite game.

Sweeping transformation: A client is working to raise the bar for how the entire market of NetSuite agencies operates, including everything from positioning to pricing to operations. He is trying to effect a somewhat broad, sweeping transformation.

Focused transformation: Another client of mine is working to help the medical device industry adopt modern software development practices. This is a transformation, but somewhat more focused than an across-the-board bar-raising.

So if you want to use your specialization to steer or transform an industry, either in a sweeping or more focused way, you'll need to be willing to embrace the risk, learning curve, and hard work of leadership. Or, you'll need to be naturally good at using the *tools* of leadership and willing to practice their use over time in service of the impact you seek.

Inspirational talks, manifestos, that kind of thing.

If your ambitions are smaller and you're using specialization not to change the world but to gain modest leverage in earning more visibility and trust for your business, you'll certainly be able to use some form of social or service trust-earning to achieve your goals. You won't be held back even if you are sure you can't make use of the leadership tools. You won't need them.

Uses for the Trust-Earning Model

Our model for trust-earning is one that has two uses. It tells us that if you want to steer or transform a market, you'd better get good at the leadership styles of trust-earning. It also informs your journey; your growth as an entrepreneurial expert.

While, again, our model is not a map showing a linear progression, it does suggest possibilities for growth. I hope it invites your mind to explore ways you might use the higher market power of leadership in service of greater positive impact on your market.

Chapter 15: Decide How to Specialize

I'm an unabashed advocate for specialization, because over and over again, I see it making the best parts of self-employment better and the worst parts less bad.

A specialization is a beachhead. You eventually move beyond it either into a deeper specialization—or alternately, a broader one—when it has served its purpose of helping you get traction and then ultimately achieve escape velocity from a situation you'd like to improve.

None of this happens if you decide but then fail to act. The decision to specialize is both easy and difficult.

Understand and Defeat The Fear

The difficult part of specializing is The Fear—a basket of related fears that surface at the worst possible moment during the specialization process. I've already touched on some of the components of The Fear.

In Chapter 8, I explained how the main risks with specialization are overevaluating the potential for harm in the specialization transition and flinching, which is exceeding your risk profile, and then hastily responding to a feeling of fear that arises during implementation.

In Chapter 9, I explained how specialization decisions are not permanent nor are they a life of renunciation and monotony. Specialization is not Mike Tyson joining a monastery.

The Fear, very unhelpfully, does not surface the moment you consider specializing. Instead, it surfaces when you are about to take action. This means you've done the decision-making work in a relatively optimistic context, and just as you're about to implement, the context suddenly changes to a pessimistic, stressful one.

This is problematic because *implementation is where specialization decisions succeed or fail*. The quality of your initial specialization decision matters, but not nearly as much as the quality of the implementation. And so, it's so *incredibly unhelpful* for The Fear to surface right before you begin the most important phase of the specialization process.

It's disorienting that The Fear surfaces at this point because you'll hear yourself saying something like: "Things were going *fine* with the specialization decision, but because of how this *feels* now that I'm about to make real changes to my business, I wonder if I actually made a bad decision."

If you've ever had a boss, you're used to having to implement someone else's bad decision from time to time. You get through it. But feeling like you're about to implement *your own* bad decision is something else entirely. It kills momentum. It makes for half-baked rather than full-throated action. And very often, it causes you to stop moving forward entirely and reevaluate the decision.

If you do that, you're screwed. The problem becomes circular and paralyzing at this point. The decision probably wasn't flawed to begin with; reevaluating it won't really help because all you'll do is come up with a different-but-not-actually-better decision that evokes *the exact same fear* when you attempt to move from the planning to the implementation phase. In other words, if you give in to The Fear, you'll get stuck in a circular fear loop. You'll think that the problem is the quality of your decision, and so you'll keep revisiting the decision, making slightly different but not-significantly-better versions of the decision and you'll feel the exact same cold, prickly fear about each one and respond by revisiting the decision. Eventually, you'll give up on specializing.

The problem is not the decision. Instead, you need to understand The Fear.

You already understand that specialization is not Mike Tyson entering a monastery. You won't find it monotonous or boring because:

- After you decide and commit to the decision, you'll feel this burst of energy and creativity because you finally know *who* you are speaking to in your marketing.

- If your technical area of focus ever becomes routine and easy, you'll enjoy the higher profitability, greater pricing power, and business scalability that leads to.

- As a small business owner, you'll always have a diverse range of stuff to deal with. Invoicing, interviewing CPAs, and evaluating new software tools are not in themselves highly fascinating activities, but they contribute to the variety of a small business owner's life.

It may, but if you also move up the value chain as you gain subject matter mastery, you'll continue to have a fresh, interesting learning curve ahead of you.

Specialization is not a life of renunciation; it is a life of engagement and growth with a narrow area of expertise within the broader, challenging, somewhat chaotic world of being a small business owner.

Imposter Syndrome's Contribution to The Fear

As you specialize, yet one more reason for you to avoid charging more for your services evaporates, leaving you alone in a room with the *real* reasons you're not charging more. For many, myself included, those reasons spring from imposter syndrome. We simply don't *feel worthy* of charging fees or rates that are actually representative of the value we create.

Imposter syndrome also surfaces before we specialize as we're mentally "trying on" the idea of calling ourselves a specialist, expert, or similar superlative. We can imagine cultivating *some* expertise, but we worry that it will be lacking in some critical way. Or we worry that if we're not extremely careful in the application of this future expertise, we'll accidentally cause harm to our clients in some way. Or we worry that our expertise is not legitimate because there's no licensing body to endorse it the way there is with physicians and other accredited professions.

Both of these facets of imposter syndrome are part of The Fear.

Loss Attention's Contribution to The Fear

The final component of The Fear is loss attention. As we're mentally trying on the idea of specialization, it's easier for us to visualize the kind of opportunities we would say no to or lose out on than it is to visualize the kind of opportunities we'll gain access to simply because we have more lived experience with the former than we do the latter. The loss is easier to visualize than the gain.

Even if the potential gain of specialization outweighs the likely loss, we can get cowed into inaction by the distorted picture of the future that loss attention produces. We can easily size up the lost revenue from the clients we will eventually say no to, but it's harder to measure the gained revenue from specialized work.

The reality of specializing is that it's a transition over time. You choose a beachhead, a specialized focus for your business. And like the smart business owner that you are, you transition your revenue base as quickly or as slowly as necessary to maintain stability during the transition. If you picked a beachhead that aligns with a strong "head start" for you, then your transition may be quite rapid. But maybe your transition is more gradual. This gives you the a chance to learn through experience what the opportunities that are available to a specialist look like. And this experience gives you the courage to let go of even more old clients and opportunities.

For me, it took about ten seconds to complete the mental aspects of this transition and about three years to execute the physical part. Ten seconds is how long it took to scan the first email I got asking me for business strategy advice after I published the first version of this book. I was immediately hooked on a new vision for how my business could create positive impact. It took three years to reposition my business in the market as a purely advisory services business and to iterate some of the core service offerings that are both unique in the market and compatible with my odd set of personal preferences.

Loss attention eventually goes away. You just need evidence that the gain is worth it, and that comes with time. The problem is that the evidence doesn't arrive until *after you start implementing your specialization decision*. The solution is to implement your decision very quickly, and prioritize marketing and sales work that will give you the quickest possible win. Chapter 17 guides you through an implementation process that prioritizes quick wins.

The Fear Is Complex and Insidious

The Fear is complex. It is made up of flawed risk analysis, overreacting to fear (flinching), overestimating the permanence of your decision, overestimating the level of monotony entailed in specializing, an unhelpful delay between deciding and feeling The Fear, imposter syndrome, and loss attention.

The Fear is also insidious; it strikes at the worst possible time—when you're moving from the important-but-easy part (the decision) to the important-and-critical part (the implementation). That's why I've spent an extravagant amount of time describing The Fear. The benefits of specialization are so compelling that I'd hate for The Fear to interfere with you obtaining them.

How to Make the Specialization Decision

There is a structured, broadly usable process for deciding how to specialize an indie consulting business. I've developed it over years of client work with hundreds of coaching clients and workshop participants. It's relevant to small services businesses where expertise plays an outsized role in value creation.

It's here: **philipmorganconsulting.com/specialization-decision-guide/**

It's on my website because it's easier to update there; print books are kind of hard to update as things change. Unlike many other business books with companion website resources, I don't ask you to provide an email address to access book resources.

In extremely brief form, the process looks like this:

1. Inventory your areas of relative advantage

2. Assess your risk profile

3. Use #1 and #2 to develop a shortlist of reasonable specialization options

4. Apply guardrails to eliminate long-shot specialization options

5. (Optional) Conduct a live market test to get feedback on your specialization decision

6. IMPLEMENT

Again, a thorough process for making this decision lives here: **philipmorganconsulting.com/specialization-decision-guide/**

Chapter 16: Sucking at Visibility and Trust-Earning Is a Huge Opportunity

Even after your specialize, you'll suck at earning visibility and trust for your services at first. That's because you're new to it. Your inexperience won't be fatal, but you won't be as good at marketing.

Specialized experts who have been doing it for a while make it look easy, creating all sorts of emotional challenges when you're starting out on a road they're well-traveled on. You compare your work to theirs and blame yourself rather than recognizing what is a natural and unavoidable learning curve.

Additionally, there's lots of bad or ill-fitting advice out there. So as you attempt to DIY your marketing, you'll try to bridge that expertise gap with advice that may not be a good fit for your context. For example, marketing that works well to sell commodities requiring little trust to purchase and little customization to use is not going to fit the context of consulting, which has completely opposite needs.

If you decide to hire a marketing firm, they will go for quick, measurable wins. Alternately, they will probably fail to grasp and communicate your expertise or the nuances that differentiate you from competitors. If they get those quick, measurable wins, they will come at the cost of tarnishing your brand, cheapening your expertise, or making you look needy.

So your choice is to suffer these forms of waste or repurpose that time, energy, and money and pursue a different approach to visibility and trust-earning.

You Have a Beautiful Opportunity

When you do anything that looks like good marketing, you are actually balancing three forms of value creation.

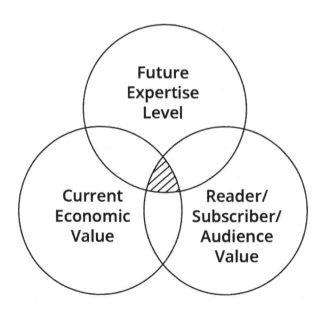

Current Economic Value: Your marketing can create short-term economic value for your business. In other words, it can help you sell your services.

Audience Value: Your marketing can create value of some kind for those it reaches. That value can range from entertainment to inspiration to information and beyond.

Future Value: Your marketing can create longer-term value for your business. The main problem with marketing in general is marketers who become distracted by a desire to create current economic value while neglecting future value creation. The best marketing focuses on future value creation in a way that also creates current economic value as a second-order consequence of the future value creation.

The very worst professional services marketing strives for efficiency over the short-term. You can maximize marketing efficiency by figuring out how to create *just barely enough* audience value to get a marketing message or call to action in front of the audience you hope to reach. Because the creation of audience value is the cost that's used to calculate the efficiency of the marketing, minimizing that cost is the usual lever that's pulled to increase efficiency/ROI.

Marketers who figure out how to create efficient, repeatable marketing tend to share their approach through blog articles, podcast interviews, etc., and this creates the idea that these approaches are best practice. They might be, if you share the goal of efficiency-at-any-cost marketing, but they won't be for long because others will copy these approaches and oversaturate the market with these copycat approaches, reducing their already borderline ability to produce audience value.

DIRECT RESPONSE MARKETING

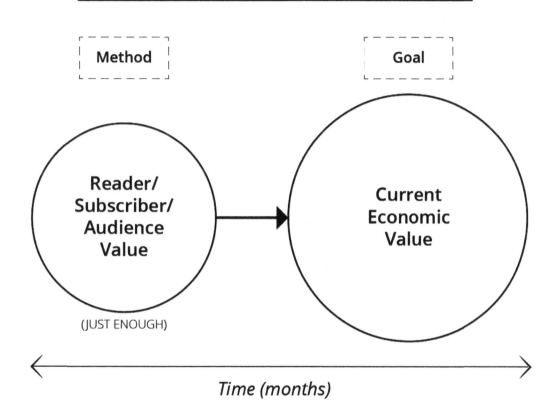

The missed opportunity with the short-term economic value-focused approach is to create long-term brand or expertise value while also creating short-term economic value as a second-order consequence. Shifting the focus to long-term value creation and trusting that this will also create short-term economic value is the opportunity that you, the person new to "doing marketing" has squarely in front of you. Here's what pursuing that opportunity looks like.

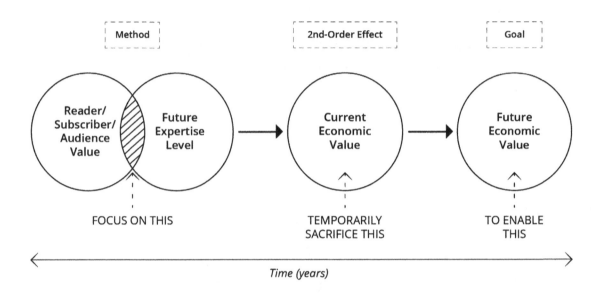

A Proposed Framework

Here's a framework that will help you take advantage of the "you suck at marketing" opportunity:

1. Publish short articles to an email list. Write and publish one article every day you work, for at least three months. If at all possible, do this writing first thing when you begin work, before you do anything at all for your clients.

2. Use the publishing in step #1 of this framework to identify an area where both you and your clients lack clarity on an important question or issue. This

will generally emerge from the publishing work somewhat naturally, though it may take longer than three months. Design and execute a micro-scale research effort to answer this question, or reduce the lack of clarity around it.

3. Self-publish the results of #2 to your audience.

That's it. You can think of this as an apprenticeship in service of your future value as an expert. You can think of it as a way to get dramatically better at marketing.

This framework puts future value at the center of everything. Rather than using publishing to sell your services, it uses publishing to cultivate your expertise and the future economic value that expertise can generate. How you do this is simple: you write and publish (to an email list) short daily articles about the intersection between what is interesting to you and what is important to your audience.

These articles can be extremely short. They can be incomplete, lacking whatever structure college professors brainwashed you into thinking is ideal. They should be daring, exploring your thinking and the edges thereof through writing.

Doing this for at least 90 days is a transformative journey. At first, you'll "feel the burn" as you struggle to keep up the daily publishing cadence. After maybe a month or so, you'll build up the needed "writing muscle" and publishing daily won't be so daunting.

Then, you'll enter the "expertise enema" phase, where you write about the topics you know the best. You are actually flushing out of your system the expertise that a future version of you will see as trivial or obvious. But you're not there yet, and this is the best you've currently got, so that's what you write about.

As the expertise enema comes to its natural conclusion, you will "hit the wall." You'll feel that you've said everything you have to say about the intersection between what is interesting to you and what is important to your audience. This moment is so incredibly important to your development as an expert, and it is very difficult emotionally. You'll face imposter syndrome and a crushing sense of discouragement at the same time. If you can push through "the wall"—keep publishing even though you are convinced that what you are writing about is complete crap—you will have developed an incredibly valuable skill; exploring important high-uncertainty domains with a consistent and persistent approach. Most schooling rewards superficial exploration of low-uncertainty domains with an inconsistent, sprint-based approach. The world has an abundant supply of this, but it needs more people who can approach high-uncertainty domains with a calm, disciplined, relentless approach. Pushing through the wall in your daily publishing practice will cultivate this skill.

After enough daily publishing, you will discover some questions that no amount of additional publishing can resolve because they are not questions that are answered by refining your thinking. They are questions that need *data*.

The Value of Data

The culture we live in has a slavish devotion to the idea of data. The *idea* of data partially frees us from the anxiety of making high-stakes decisions (or decisions that we imagine have high stakes). The idea of data promises to make a huge and overwhelmingly complex world into something comprehensible. The idea of data helps us feel powerful.

The reality is that data is one tool among many that can accomplish what we seek. If uncertainty reduction is the goal, trial-and-error, mentorship, or even dumb luck can get us from a high to a relatively lower degree of uncertainty about something. If anxiety reduction is the goal, then learning, meditation, or medication can get us at least part of the way there.

But again, our culture worships data, and so learning to use data in service of your clients is worthwhile. The latter two parts of The Expertise Incubator framework focus on small-scale data collection.

The first and most important thing here is mindset: *you are using data to help your clients make better decisions.* That desire must guide your work.

The second most important thing here is scope: the question you seek to answer must be *tiny*. If you get too ambitious with the scope of your research question, it will overwhelm you with complexity or scale or both and lead to discouragement or failure. Pursuing the answer to a tiny question won't feel like an impressive task, but *finding* a defensible answer to a tiny question that nobody in your industry has a good answer to will revolutionize your business because it will lead to bigger and better versions of this kind of research.

Guillaume is also used as an example in Chapter 13.

Here's an example. Guillaume makes a good living helping start-ups use strategic storytelling to increase employee alignment and gain traction in the market. As he was writing and publishing about this topic three times per week to his email list, he began to ask himself forbidden questions: Does strategic storytelling even work? Does it produce a return on investment? Does it live up to the claims made about its impact?

If the idea of strategic storytelling is new to you, the talk "How great leaders inspire action" by Simon Sinek is a reasonably good introduction to the broader idea of using storytelling or a narrative to increase employee alignment and gain traction in the market.

These are forbidden questions because most consultants who offer services connected to strategic storytelling aren't interested in uncovering what would become in inconvenient truth if they discovered there's no robust evidence that their work produces ROI. And there are enough prospects out there who are willing to speculatively invest in strategic storytelling consulting in the hopes that it will do something good for their business. Lots of folks in this market are happy to, to paraphrase Nigel Tufnel, leave this mystery unsolved.

Guillaume was willing to ask the questions because the answer would serve his clients, and he's okay with pivoting elsewhere if he discovers there's no robust evidence of ROI for his chosen methodology. His research process begins like this:

1. Reduce the scope of the question from "Does strategic storytelling product ROI?" to something much, much smaller.

2. Conduct a literature review to further inform and refine the question in #1, avoid a duplicative research effort, and learn from the methodologies that may have been used before.

3. a. If the literature review was sufficiently informative, Guillaume's first research product might be some analysis of what he found during the literature review.

   b. The literature review might not answer the question Guillaume has, so he might move on to the next step—designing and executing primary research.

As you move into doing primary research, there are several additional ideas that are critical:

- **Your goal is not certainty; your goal is the reduction of uncertainty**. You may never get a complete, irrefutable answer to your question, but you can get useful data that assists with your clients' decision-making.

  Credit to Douglas Hubbard for popularizing this idea.

- **Small data sets can be useful**. You are not trying to determine the efficacy of a vaccine, design a nuclear reactor, or advise a government on public policy, so you do not need the levels of scientific rigor associated with those projects. This is not an invitation to be intentionally sloppy, but an invitation to gather, analyze, and use data to serve your clients without unreasonable encumbrances.

At this point, this Expertise Incubator framework idea is either intriguing to you or too far out there to consider. Either outcome is fine, but if you find the idea intriguing, I have published a series of 18 videos on YouTube exploring it further. Search for "TEI Talks" on youtube.com and you should be able to easily find them.

Get Where You're Going by Walking Cowpaths

It is said that Boston's streets were once meandering cowpaths that developed over time into roads. This isn't actually true, but the idea of wandering around the intersection between what is interesting to you and what is important to your audience is a powerful one.

If you've specialized, you do not need a "content marketing plan." Instead, you need to publish a lot in a medium that facilitates conversations. An email list is ideal for this. Beyond that, you only need to explore what is both interesting to you and important to your audience. The mechanics of publishing daily will do the rest.

You will wander around what feel like cowpaths. This process is, in the short-term, wasteful, but only in the way that actors rehearsing their lines is wasteful. When the "cameras are rolling," you hit your lines almost effortlessly because of this cowpathing.

The practice of frequent publishing makes you frighteningly good at using high-impact marketing (speaking, podcast guesting, etc.) in a powerful, fluent way. If you follow this advice, you'll spend a year or two preparing to do marketing in a way that is far less likely to tarnish your brand or diminish your expertise. After this, you can effectively hire help or DIY it in a much more effective way.

Remember, the opportunity of being bad at marketing is to *not* do conventional marketing at all and instead repurpose marketing tools to *develop valuable expertise that few others are willing to work hard to develop.*

Chapter 17: The Mechanics of Earning Visibility and Trust

Know what's better than deciding you want to specialize, choosing a specialization, changing your website to match, and then getting an inquiry from a great-fit prospect a few weeks later?

Here's what's better: deciding you want to specialize, choosing a specialization, changing your website to match, and then getting an inquiry from a great-fit prospect a few *days* later.

Feedback from the market is so valuable because it clarifies your direction, fortifies you, and helps you keep going. The faster you can get it, the better.

I recently spoke with a prospect who decided on a new specialized focus, changed his website to match, and got an excited inquiry from a good-fit prospect *the same day* the website went live. That almost never happens, and that's not where we set the bar for sufficiently rapid market feedback.

"Fastest" is measured in relative terms in the context of your project length and other "business metabolism" factors, not in absolute terms like days/weeks/months.

The orientation toward speed, however, is important during the early phase of implementing a specialization decision. You want the fastest possible time to feedback from the market because of the emotional benefits that rapid feedback provides. There's less sunk cost to deal with, and less time to experience the anxiety that uncertainty produces. You can't control things like inbound lead volume. But you *can* eliminate unnecessary time-wasting activity as you move into implementing your specialization decision.

I want to remind you that all of the advice in this book is tailored for the solo indie consultant or the very small expertise-driven services business. And further, it's all advice that assumes you're specializing for the first time. If you're re-specializing, or if you already have momentum as a specialist, then the advice that follows is less relevant for you.

A Specialization Implementation Recipe

I normally offer frameworks, not recipes, but here's a useful recipe for starting to implement your specialization decision:

1. **Contact all your current clients** and let them know about your new specialization. Unless you want them to panic-quit you, lay out a transition plan for them. That plan could include working with them for as long as they need. It could be a more rapid transition away from working with you. Do whatever fits your goals, context, and risk profile. Make sure they feel heard and listened to during this conversation.

The more human and high-bandwidth you can make this communication, the better. A realtime voice/video conversation is generally the gold standard here.

2. **Contact all your previous clients** and let them know about the new specialization. Less high-bandwidth approaches are fine here. Let them know that if they want to help you, they could search their "mental Rolodex" for introductions they could make that might fit the new specialized focus.

3. **Update all your social media accounts/properties** with the new focus. Be as clear, simple, and un-clever as possible in how you word things.

4. **Update your website** as quickly as possible.

Step #4 in this recipe can kill you. Not literally, but it is the place where you are most likely to conduct a dramatic reenactment of the healthcare.gov debacle but on your own website. Please don't.

You might need a great website, but what you need more *now* in the very early phases of the specialization implementation is a *functional website* that clearly describes who your business serves, what you do for them, and a few other relevant details. One website page and a few hundred words of copy on that site are usually enough. You can and should revisit the website after you have made headway on the rest of this recipe.

5. **Consider The Expertise Incubator framework** described in the previous chapter, especially if you have the ability to execute a more gradual transition to your new specialization. This will often delay getting feedback from the market, but it will enable other worthwhile things, so it can be a good tradeoff.

6. **If you want or need to get a *response* from your new specialized focus quicker**, you need to use faster-acting tools.

Conversations are what will quickly lead to the traction you need. This is true even if you are an introvert. This is true if your service is simple. This is true if your service is complex. This is true if your service is cheap. Or expensive. It is almost universally true within the world of consulting services.

Sales matter too, of course. They matter a lot. But conversations precede sales, even if you imagine a future where the selling is product-like or low-cost. In the very early days of a new specialization, optimize for conversations. As you do so, favor simple, low-tech tools.

Simple, low-tech tools for earning visibility, connection, and trust from an audience include:

- Anything that **leverages an existing authoritative publication** (trade publications, someone else's podcast or event, etc.) for getting your thinking in front of your target market.

- **Email list**. Don't allow yourself to use fancy segmentation, lead scoring, personalization, or complex digital marketing funnels until you get a comment from at least 10 strangers on the strength of your expertise or point of view. Generally avoid using urgency, fear of missing out, or fear-baiting.

- Anything that relies on **RSS** for distributing content. This includes a blog, hosting a podcast, or guesting on others' podcast.

- **Curated, small group realtime interaction** with those from whom you are trying to earn visibility and trust. It's okay if the tech that facilitates this is somewhat complex as long as the experience for participants is intimate and high quality. It's fine if you're listening to them, learning from them, speaking to them from a stage, teaching them, or demonstrating expertise for them. All are trust-building forms of interaction. Selling aggressively to them as a group is not.

- Make use of a **social media platform** to share your thinking. Considered alone, social media is not usually a valuable method for earning visibility and trust, but it is cheap, relatively easy to use, and in some cases, very fast-acting, so it's worth considering using at this point in your specialization journey.

- **If possible, use outreach to facilitate conversations**. Horizontal specializations are generally incompatible with outreach visibility methods, but outreach can work fine with vertical or service specializations. Outreach can be fast-acting, effective, and cheap. That is why bottom-feeding services businesses have started using it so heavily for sales. Do not join their ranks. Outreach combined with a willingness to do the emotional labor of caring about those you are reaching out to will always be a usable visibility-increasing tool.

Other Helpful Assets

There are a few more assets that will help you implement your specialization decision:

- Ecosystem of support

- Time

- Patience, discipline, and courage

Eventually, you'll need an ecosystem of support. One of the ways you can cultivate the reputation you want is to recruit the help of certain people. These include:

- People who can refer you when the right kind of prospective client asks them for a referral.

- People who can get you in front of their audience and help you connect with the right kind of prospective clients.

- People who can call attention to your work because it's relevant to their audience.

- People who have a complementary product or service who can refer you to their customers or clients.

- People who admire your work and spread the word without you asking them.

One of my coaching clients is cultivating a relationship with a *Wall Street Journal* (*WSJ*) reporter whose beat (the intersection of tech, business, and culture) overlaps with my client's focus. My client is playing the long game of slow, gradual engagement, starting with social media interaction. Eventually, this *WSJ* reporter will be part of my client's ecosystem of support. I don't know exactly how or when, but I call this out here because it's a good example of what I mean by an ecosystem of support. You can run your business alone, but you can't reach the highest possible level of success without other people.

Cultivating an ecosystem of support is something you can do intentionally, but it's not something you can develop a granular, precise plan for. It's much more about keeping an ear to the ground for beneficial relationships and opportunity, and then taking action when they present themselves.

The final group of assets you'll need to implement a specialization decision: time, patience, discipline, and courage. They go together because they are the human stuff—the grit and heart—that you bring to the process. They are vital ingredients in the asset you are trying to build.

The Importance of Speed and Conversations

This is as close to a recipe as you're going to get from me, and I am happy to admit it's more like a typical pound cake recipe than a precise recipe for a delicate French pastry.

Building a marketing platform takes time and experimentation. There's no single recipe you can follow that will work for every independent consultant. Building it takes real work.

Remember that speed is critical. Direct response marketing tools are the right ones for speed. Eventually, their use will impose a trust ceiling, though, so be ready to drop or reduce your usage of those tools later.

Remember that conversations are critical. Optimize your marketing to generate conversations. Sales will follow, but the market feedback you get from conversations is more important early on.

Favor simple, low-tech tools wherever possible. A lot of SaaS companies make good money by convincing you that the source of the vaguely sad, disappointed feeling you have when thinking about your marketing is inadequate tooling. The real source of that feeling is that you haven't learned how to use marketing to improve the lives of a small number of people. Better tools won't help with this learning curve.

After you've decided how you will specialize, you'll find that some of the difficult or confusing parts of building a marketing platform have become easier to figure out. You'll have more clarity about who you need to reach, and you'll have better ideas about how to reach them. This new clarity makes beginning the work of building a marketing platform easier.

Chapter 18: Shine on, You Crazy Diamond

I threw away a 59,000-word draft of this book and rewrote from scratch the version you've hopefully just finished reading. This version is half the length because of something I realized about you and me while writing the first version.

You're so much more likely to succeed and thrive than I was giving you credit for in that first discarded draft.

That *is* what I want for you: thriving success; using your business as a lever to enable a growing, rewarding, thriving, interesting life. My personality tends to surround dreams and goals with a thick layer of *anxiety* about de-risking the pursuit of those things. The first draft of this book was probably about 20K to 30K words of useful guidance and 30K to 40K words of anxiety-driven "watch out for this!" details and caveats and . . . well, let's just call it *friction* that would have hindered you in implementing a very good idea— specialization—in your business.

You're so much more capable and creative than I was giving you credit for in that first friction-laden draft. This version has, I hope, given you the essence of the ideas and models you need to transform your business without any unneeded cruft or helicopter-parenting- style coddling.

These ideas are simple, but powerful.

1. We will run into a ceiling on our ability to earn visibility and trust. This will create a ceiling on the opportunities we have access to.

2. Specialization is choosing and leveraging a beachhead to break through this ceiling. Beachheads are an important, but temporary, part of a larger strategy.

3. With specialization, strive to decide well, but make sure you implement even better than you decide. To paraphrase Drucker, implementation eats decision-making for breakfast.

4. Know thine enemy. The Fear is the feeling of exceeding your comfort zone disguised as doubt about your decision-making ability.

5. Marketing is how you earn new levels of visibility and trust. It is also how you initiate conversations and make enough memories in the market that hearing your name creates a warm, trust-y feeling among those in the market.

Sail on, you bold entrepreneurial expert!

Shine on, you crazy diamond.

About the Author

Philip Morgan's work on specialization, cultivating expertise, and monetizing IP helps independent consultants thrive.

He has helped thousands of indie consultants use specialization to find a beachhead that leads to greater visibility, profitability, expertise, and success.

He's also fascinated by those who cultivate valuable self-made expertise outside the narrow confines of licensed professions, and he constructs group challenges and experiential learning experiences that help his clients cultivate this kind of expertise.

He was born in the U.S. Virgin Islands and has been searching his whole life, without satisfaction, for a commercial ginger beer that matches the fiery home-brewed ginger beer he tasted there.

After living in 28 different houses in five states and the aforementioned U.S. territory, he seems to be settling down in Taos, New Mexico, with an incredibly understanding wife and two Ragdoll cats.

He enjoys hiking, snowshoeing, black and white photography, and building horn and open-baffle speaker systems.

indieexperts.io

philipmorganconsulting.com

philip@philipmorganconsulting.com

Credits

Locations: A plywood shack in Sebastopol, CA, an adobe casita in Taos, NM, and Yerba Canyon in Carson National Forest

Editing: Heather Pendley, pendleysproediting.com

Illustrations: Volha Khamitsevich

Author Photo: Cheryl Janis

Author Assistance: Alarm clock + Hario V60 + 30g of Ethiopia Sidma light roast + Baratza Encore on 16 + 330g just-off-boil water

Made in the USA
Coppell, TX
16 September 2021